"This wonderful volume he [...] mon heart issue by carefully and comprehensively walking us through biblical teaching and examples that show how the grace of God in Christ can enable us to overcome bitterness. It often reads like a good biblical counseling session and will be of great help to both counselors and counselees."

> **Dr. Jim Newheiser**, director of the Christian Counseling Program at Reformed Theological Seminary, Charlotte; executive director of the Institute for Biblical Counseling and Discipleship

"Pastor Steve's latest offering, *Overcoming Bitterness*, tackles a much-needed but oft-neglected topic. People from all walks of life can carry and harbor pockets of bitterness, and we can all too frequently ignore the fruit of bitterness in our life. With a pastor's heart and a counselor's skill, Viars brings biblical clarity and practical counsel for this common issue. Readers will be surprised, encouraged, and convicted by the helpful counsel contained in this brief book. I commend it to you heartily!"

> **Jonathan D. Holmes**, pastor of counseling, Parkside Church; executive director, Fieldstone Counseling

"This book brims with hope for the bitter person and for those who live with them. This will be an extremely helpful resource for biblical counselors."

> **Randy Patten**, Director of Training Emeritus, Association of Certified Biblical Counselors; president, TEAM Focus Ministries

"In *Overcoming Bitterness*, Pastor Steve Viars provides practical biblical counsel for an issue that everyone faces at one time or another. Yet, few of us truly understand bitterness biblically. Steve artfully, compassionately, and comprehensively addresses bitterness both as a lament over suffering to be brought to our caring Father and as a heart issue of sin to be brought to our forgiving Savior. *Overcoming Bitterness* will be a wonderfully beneficial equipping tool for individuals and small groups, and for pastors and counselors."

Bob Kellemen, academic dean, Faith Bible Seminary; author of over twenty books, including *God's Healing for Life's Losses*

"Guiding people to see bitterness from behavioral, conditional, and heart perspectives is brilliant! Dr. Viars writes with the precision of a theologian and the practicality of a pastor. This is a great read and very helpful for people who truly want to address bitterness."

Dr. Nicolas Ellen, senior pastor of Community of Faith Bible Church, and senior professor of biblical counseling at the College of Biblical Studies, Houston, TX

OVERCOMING
BITTERNESS

OVERCOMING BITTERNESS

MOVING FROM LIFE'S GREATEST HURTS TO A LIFE FILLED WITH JOY

STEPHEN VIARS

BakerBooks

a division of Baker Publishing Group
Grand Rapids, Michigan

Published by Baker Books
a division of Baker Publishing Group
PO Box 6287, Grand Rapids, MI 49516-6287
www.bakerbooks.com

Printed in the United States of America

Library of Congress Cataloging-in-Publication Data
Names: Viars, Stephen, 1960– author.
Title: Overcoming bitterness : moving from life's greatest hurts to a life filled with joy / Stephen Viars.
Description: Grand Rapids, Michigan : Baker Books, a division of Baker Publishing Group, 2021. | Includes bibliographical references.
Identifiers: LCCN 2020018545 | ISBN 9781540900630 (paperback) | ISBN 9781540901514 (casebound)
Subjects: LCSH: Disappointment—Religious aspects—Christianity. | Regret—Religious aspects—Christianity. | Jealousy—Religious aspects—Christianity. | Resentment.
Classification: LCC BV4909 .V525 2020 | DDC 248.8/6—dc23
LC record available at https://lccn.loc.gov/2020018545

21 22 23 24 25 26 27   7 6 5 4 3 2 1

To my wife, Kris, and our son, the Bear.

You both have faced adversity
by choosing joy in Christ.
By avoiding sinful bitterness,
you have been an example to many
and a rich blessing to me.

Contents

1

This Problem Is Bigger Than We Think

Imagine you're having coffee with a friend who knows you well, and during the course of the conversation they ask you, "Do you have any bitterness in your life?" How would you answer them? While admittedly this is not the kind of question we generally contemplate while standing in line at a fast-food restaurant, it is certainly worth considering in a more reflective moment. Do you have any bitterness in your life?

You Better Believe I Do!

As a pastor, I've been in enough of these kinds of conversations over the years to know that the responses can be rich and varied. Some people become animated as they tell about their unfair or harsh treatment by someone in their past, and then conclude by proclaiming, "You better believe I'm bitter, and I have every right to be!"

No pretension there. However, if you know the Bible well, you can probably think of statements to suggest that way of living might be displeasing to God. For example, Paul told the Christians in Ephesus, "Let all bitterness and wrath and anger and clamor and slander be put away from you, along with all malice. Be kind to one another, tender-hearted, forgiving each other, just as God in Christ also has forgiven you" (Eph. 4:31–32).

The truth is that unrestrained bitterness will destroy us. As author Lee Strobel explains, "Acrid bitterness inevitably seeps into the lives of people who harbor grudges and suppress anger, and bitterness is always a poison. It keeps your pain alive instead of letting you deal with it and get beyond it. Bitterness sentences you to relive the hurt over and over."[1]

An unknown author noted that "bitterness does more harm to the vessel in which it is stored than the vessel on which it is poured." Many of us can tell stories from personal experience of how that statement is painfully true.

The costs of not addressing this issue are high and varied. Some people try to self-medicate with drugs and alcohol in an attempt to dull the pain. Others turn to shallow and illicit sexual relationships to find meaning and happiness in a new person or experience. Bitterness is often connected to anxiety, worry, depression, and fear. Marriages dissolve and families disintegrate if bitterness is left unaddressed. The Bible warns against unrestrained bitterness, because the God of heaven does not want anyone to suffer these terrible effects.

No, Not at All?

On the other hand, perhaps you're the kind of person who would say, "I've progressed in my relationship with the Lord to where I'm trying to rid my heart and life of unrestrained bitterness because I know how damaging it can be to my walk with Christ." That's wonderful, but it doesn't mean you or anyone else could say, "No, I don't have any bitterness in my life at all." In the following pages, I will show that such a position is simply not possible. This side of heaven, we all have bitterness.

Three Distinct Categories

One benefit of studying the Word of God is that it brings clarity and understanding. That's why those who identify as followers of Jesus Christ view the Bible as a lamp unto our feet and a light unto our path (Ps. 119:105). We want to know everything the Bible says about various topics.

The word "bitter" is generally translated in our English Bibles from the Old Testament Hebrew word *marah* and the New Testament Greek word *pikros*. Sometimes these terms are used literally to speak of food or water that tastes sour, acrid, or bitter—the opposite of something sweet. This picturesque word group is even used to describe the "poisonous putrid bile from the gall bladder, the gall bladder itself (Job 16:13; 20:25) or the poison of snakes (Job 20:14)."[2] Often, God's Word uses it figuratively to speak of "inner emotional feeling of deep sorrow or an outwardly directed anger that cries out."[3] Isn't it amazing that God loves us so much that he uses such a powerful word to help us understand the importance of addressing this issue in our lives?

When we begin to examine the various ways these words occur in the Bible, we may be surprised to learn that God speaks to us about three very different kinds of bitterness.

The Poison of a Bitter Lifestyle

A bitter lifestyle is what is most recognizable—call it full-on bitterness. I'm thinking here about passages like the one quoted above from Ephesians 4:31–32 that describe this subject in terms of behavior you can readily observe. Later, we will see how this kind of bitterness might even affect a person's appearance over time. Can you think of a person in your life who looks bitter? Perhaps more to the point, is that ever the person you see in the mirror in the morning?

The writer of Hebrews warns that if left unattended, this kind of bitter lifestyle can result in being an "immoral or godless person like Esau, who sold his own birthright for a single meal" (12:16). He then explains where that path leads: "For you know that even afterwards, when he desired to inherit the blessing, he was rejected, for he found no place for repentance, though he sought for it with tears" (12:17).

What a haunting possibility—no place for repentance. We will talk later about what that phrase probably means, but can we all agree at this point that however you interpret it, it is very, very bad? I hope we would all say, "I want to do everything in my power—and by that I mean through the power of the Savior who works within me—to avoid ever being in any way like Esau."

You can view this kind of behavioral bitterness like the top of a logjam in a river. Too many Christians have allowed this characteristic to hinder their relationships, their effectiveness, and their joy. One of our goals in this book is to apply the dynamite of God's Word at the appropriate places in the logjam so you can overcome these kinds of words and actions. If that's necessary in your particular situation, then sit back and let the blasting begin.

The Power of a Bitter Heart

However, what's happening on the outside is not the sum of what the Bible says about this subject. Scripture also affirms that "the heart knows its own bitterness" (Prov. 14:10). You don't make bitterness in the microwave. Instead you slow-cook it in the Crock-Pot of your heart as you replay frustrations and disappointments and hurts over and over.

Bitterness, like many other topics in the Bible, involves a constant interplay between the hands and the heart, or between the mouth and the heart. Perhaps it shouldn't surprise us that in one of the Bible's most extended explanations about the power of the tongue, we find the subject of bitterness mixed into the discussion. James chastises his readers because "from the same mouth come both blessing and cursing. My brethren, these things ought not to be this way. Does a fountain send out from the same opening both fresh and bitter water?" (James 3:10–11). In other words, examine the source that is producing the bitter words.

There are a number of lessons in this passage about the tongue that we will address in a later chapter, but the point here is this: we won't do this subject justice, biblically speaking, unless we look not just at the behavioral logjam but also at what may be building up beneath the surface in our heart.

I was recently talking to a friend who owns a cabin on a lake, and he was telling me he had been working to free a downed log that was stuck under his dock. He explained that after he disengaged the log, he tied it off to a neighbor's tree on the shore. His concern was that downed trees could become waterlogged and lurk just below the surface, becoming potentially catastrophic for boaters and skiers. Lake residents call them "deadheads." Sometimes that condition, spiritually speaking, can be worse than a visible logjam. That's why the Bible says we should "watch over [our] heart with all diligence, for from it flow the springs of life" (Prov. 4:23).

Recall the fascinating example of this interplay between the inner and outer person in Acts 8. The church is in its earliest days, and the apostles are laying their hands on new ethnic groups of Christ followers who then receive the gift of the Holy Spirit. A man named Simon approaches them and offers to buy the power and authority to do the same thing.

The apostle Peter, never one to mince words, says, "May your silver perish with you, because you thought you could obtain the gift of God with money! You have no part or portion in this matter, for your heart is not right before God" (Acts 8:20–21). Clearly, Peter's ultimate concern is not just the outrageous nature of Simon's request but the deeper issue of what this offer reveals about his unconverted heart. Peter goes on to drive this point home by admonishing Simon, "Therefore repent of this wickedness of yours, and pray the Lord that, if possible, the intention of your heart may be forgiven you" (8:22).

Then Peter makes a diagnosis of Simon's inner man that ought to get our attention: "For I see that you are in the gall of bitterness and in the bondage of iniquity" (8:23). A statement like that raises as many questions as it answers, because Peter doesn't explain—at least not in what is recorded for us in God's Word—how or why Simon is bitter. However, we have enough information before us to ask this piercing question: Would God ever have reason to speak similar words to you or me?

PULL OVER AND PARK

If you enjoy road trips or long journeys, you know that occasionally it is best to pull over and park. Maybe you're tired and need a break. Sometimes you need to pause and focus on your written instructions to guide your next steps. Throughout this book, we will do that together with the goal of reaching our destination of overcoming bitterness in the power of the gospel.

This is a good time to set the book aside and reach for a piece of paper or an electronic device and make a list of anything happening in your life that would fall under these first two categories. What examples of bitterness are occurring in your words or actions? What examples of bitter thoughts or desires are present in your heart?

This aspect of bitterness is like the underside of the logjam we mentioned earlier. It is where the limbs can be more tangled and sometimes even caked with mud and debris. However, the dynamite of God's Word works equally well under the water. Be encouraged that "the word of God is living and active and sharper than any two-edged sword, and piercing as far as the division of soul and spirit, of both joints and marrow, and able to judge the thoughts and intentions of the heart" (Heb. 4:12). Bitterness can even be overcome at the level of the heart.

The Presence of Bitter Conditions

As I researched this subject, the first two categories were not surprising. As someone who has provided biblical counseling to people in the church and community for over thirty years, I'm used to seeing Scripture navigate our attention between the inner and outer person. However, I wasn't expecting to see the significant and powerful ways the Word of God also discusses bitterness as a condition. In other words, it is not just a *response*, it is a *reality*.

People can treat us in all sorts of ways that the Bible would call bitter. The subject is so robust in God's Word that we will devote the entire next chapter to unpacking it more fully. However, please allow this initial salvo to sink deeply into your heart. This topic does not start with what you *do*. No one has ever gotten out of bed and decided, "I think I'll just get up and start being bitter at no particular person for no particular reason." Even if the reality is more of something that was perceived than what actually occurred—in that person's mind, that's what happened.

Here is why that's so important: the Word of God has a very rich and robust theology of suffering to help us respond well to bitter circumstances. But if we simply run to verses like Philippians 4:4—"Rejoice in the Lord always, again I say rejoice"—and repeat it over and over, we will ignore great portions of Scripture that help us process pain and hurt and abuse and injustice well.

I've been reading a book by David McCullough titled *The Pioneers*. I love McCullough's treatment of various periods of American history and often end my days in my leather chair next to the fireplace with one of his books in hand.

This particular volume is about the early settlers of Marietta, Ohio. It is a delightful story, including accounts of the godly men and women whose Christian faith caused them to insist that slavery would never be practiced in their state.

One of the Ohio patriarchs was Ephraim Cutler, a man who along with his family had an incredibly powerful and Christlike impact on their state. However, at a touching point in the story, McCullough records:

> In the early spring of 1849, Ephraim's oldest son, Charles, announced he was joining the rush to California for gold. "A year ago we had not <u>heard</u> of the gold of California, and even after the papers were filled with descriptions of the immense regions where it is found, and of the multitudes who went to seek it—It never occurred to me that any one dear to us would go there," wrote Julia [Charles' sister]. Again, as in her father's earlier days, the west was the future.
>
> Two months later came word from California that Charles had died of cholera. The news shook the whole family in a way nothing had—"to think of his dying away from home and friends, buried upon those vast plains where no one knows even the place of his last rest," Julia wrote. And the blow fell hardest on Ephraim. "He is very much bowed down under the stroke—still he murmurs not, the language of his heart seems to be, 'I was dumb. I opened not my mouth, because thou God dids't it.' Occasionally we hear a suppressed groan as he walks his room with clasped hands."[4]

What a sad story of a broken father dealing with unspeakable grief. It is especially fascinating that his daughter Julia explained her father's lack of talking about what was occurring inside his breaking heart by quoting Psalm 39:9—"I have become mute, I do not open my mouth, because it is You who have done it."

The problem is that such an interpretation and application of that verse ignores the context of Psalm 39. In verse 1, David explains his hesitancy to speak: "I will guard my ways that I may not sin with my tongue; I will guard my mouth as with a muzzle while the wicked are in my presence." David wants to be sure that he utters his authentic expressions of pain and sorrow only to God and to the appropriate persons, because those who do not know the Lord might twist what he says to justify their own unbelief. He even affirms in verse 2 that while he remained "mute and silent," his "sorrow grew worse."

That's why in the remainder of this beautiful psalm of lament, David records how he speaks openly to God about his pain. For example, in verses 3–4, he proclaims, "My heart was hot within me, while I was musing the fire burned; then I spoke with my tongue: 'LORD, make me to know my end and what is the extent of my days; let me know how transient I am.'"

I feel badly for the many people who, like Ephraim Cutler, somewhere along the line have adopted the position that choosing to follow Jesus Christ resigns you to a life of suffering in impassionate, stoic silence. Nothing could be further from the truth. Please hear this: *being unable or unwilling to speak in the right way, at the right time, to the right people about the bitter circumstances of life is not an antidote but an accelerant to a bitter heart and life.* In other words, how you handle bitter circumstances will either lead to or prevent a bitter response in both the inner and outer person.

If you simply ignore the hurt, the pain, or the disappointment, you may not see the visible logjam of bitter words and actions—at least not right away. You may not yet have the submerged log under the surface of a bitter heart. However, the inability to properly process bitter circumstances will invariably produce a gradual shallowness in your stream. That unaddressed sadness, hurt, and grief will be like silt that builds up over time. Maybe you won't immediately see it from the surface, but your river of faith and vibrancy will become shallower with each passing year. What is needed here is not so much a stick of dynamite but a steam shovel. You have to find a way to dig down and dredge out that silt and debris and make the river flow clearly and deeply again—perhaps deeper than ever.

The Goal We Are Pursuing

The purpose of this book is to help you overcome bitterness. I have had the privilege of serving at the same church for over thirty years now. Many of the men and women in our church and community are delightful people.

However, I have also watched bitterness destroy people's faith, health, family, and testimony. It is often the antithesis of spiritual growth and health. This is why the apostle Paul places bitterness alongside wrath, anger, clamor, and evil speaking in opposition to being kind, tender-hearted, and forgiving. My goal in this book is to help you deal with bitterness thoroughly and completely in a way that helps you bask in the sweetness of our Savior.

Organizing Our Study

The three classifications of bitterness that we have reviewed in this chapter will form the framework for the rest of the book. We will first learn to face the *reality* of bitterness. What does it look like to avoid the stoic tendencies of well-meaning people like Ephraim Cutler? How can followers of Jesus Christ learn to suffer well so that our response to bitter circumstances takes us in directions that honor the Lord?

Then we will pivot to the sinful and personal *responsibility* side of the equation and find ways to avoid the pitfalls that lead to a bitter heart and life. If you conclude you have already fallen into one or more of those pits, we will also discuss plenty of ladders of God's grace and strength to climb out and find sweet, solid ground.

In the final third of our time together, we will put all our principles to the test by examining a delightful case study of a woman whose life was consumed with bitterness. It even affected her appearance, to the point that she asked her friends to replace her given name with the word that described her best: bitter. Imagine telling those around you, "Just call me bitter." The good news is, the story doesn't end there. Not even close. Not surprisingly, our sweet Savior is visible in ways that will take your breath away.

One Final Thought

This book is written for people who have placed their faith and trust in Jesus Christ as Savior and Lord. However, I realize you may have picked up this book even though you don't consider yourself a Christian. Can I tell you something? As I wrote, I specifically prayed for people just like you. My guess is that you have a hard story to tell—why else would you be interested in this topic?

I hope that, as you consider what the Word of God says about the bad events in your life, you will eventually be open to thinking about the ultimate news the Bible says is very, very good. It is called the gospel, the good news that Jesus Christ died on the cross in the bitterest way so that you and I could admit our sin, accept his free gift of forgiveness and grace, and establish a vibrant, personal relationship with him. Friend, Jesus Christ is the embodiment of sweetness. I hope this study convinces you of that delightful truth.

» QUESTIONS FOR PERSONAL REFLECTION

1. How did you answer the question posed at the beginning of this chapter: "Do you have any bitterness in your life?" Is your answer any different now?

2. Of the three categories of bitterness we have studied—the poison of a bitter lifestyle, the power of a bitter heart, and the presence of bitter conditions—which has been most prevalent in your past? Which is most prevalent in your life today?

3. Write out your story of bitterness. What have been the bitterest circumstances? How did you process what occurred? How, if at all, did you cross the line into bitter patterns of thinking and desiring? How, if at all, did you cross the line into bitter words and actions?

» QUESTIONS FOR GROUP DISCUSSION

1. In your social circles, how prevalent is bitterness? How and in what ways is that true?

2. Share an example of bitterness in your life with your group. What happened? How did your bitterness feel? How did it think? What did it want? How did it sound? What did it do?

3. What questions do you hope to answer with this study? What do you desire to happen in your life and with the other group members as you walk through this material together?

2

The Presence of Bitter Conditions

I often begin each day in my favorite chair, reading and medi-
tating on the Bible. Many times, I find myself responding
with surprise to something the Lord says or does. There are
constant reminders that his thoughts are not my thoughts
and his ways are not my ways (Isa. 55:8–9). As a result, my
perspective on life is expanded and altered so I am better
prepared to serve my Lord that day.

This is especially true when you examine what Scripture
says about the subject of bitterness. As we learned in chapter
1, God uses picturesque language to grab our attention with
the Old Testament word *marah* and the New Testament
word *pikros*. These terms describe something that tastes sour
or brackish—the polar opposite of sweet. One dictionary of
Old Testament words even defines the word group as "the
poisonous putrid bile from the gall bladder" and "an inner
emotional feeling of deep sorrow or an outwardly directed
anger that cries out to the power that seems to be causing

the problem."[1] We all know that taste. More to the point, we all know that feeling.

Then the Lord throws a curveball. Bitterness is not just a response, it is also a reality. Some of the Bible's most powerful uses of this word group speak about the harsh conditions of living in a fallen world. Biblically speaking, bitterness is not simply something you do—it is something you experience.

Face Your Bitter Circumstances

I wonder if many of us have been so conditioned by a watered-down "just be joyful" version of Christianity that we are practically incapable of acknowledging aspects of our lives that are being played out in the minor key. We may have even convinced ourselves that talking about trials and disappointments will lead to a bitter heart and lifestyle. What if the exact opposite is true? Perhaps Scripture uses the word "bitter" to describe some of our past or present circumstances so we will face them head-on before we cross the line into sinful bitterness of heart and life. If that's the case—and I strongly believe it is—we will benefit from this surprising message from God's Word. Bitterness is not just a response; it is a reality.

Jealous Attacks

One of the fascinating places where the Bible uses the word "bitter" to describe someone's condition is in Genesis 49. This is where the patriarch Jacob (who was renamed Israel) gathers his sons around his deathbed and makes a series of amazing statements and prophecies. We read, "Then Jacob summoned his sons and said, 'Assemble yourselves that I may tell you what will befall you in the days to come. Gather together and hear, O sons of Jacob; and listen to Israel your father'" (Gen. 49:1–2).

Surely, this will be a time to ignore skeletons in the family closet. Jacob won't encourage his sons to face any negative choices they had made or experienced at such a tender moment as this, will he? The answer comes quickly when he tells his firstborn son, Reuben, "Uncontrolled as water, you shall not have preeminence" (Gen. 49:4). Anyone old enough to remember trying to carry an ice cube tray from the kitchen faucet to the freezer without spilling a substantial portion can visualize the metaphor. That was Reuben—unstable as water.

Jacob goes on to describe son after son with a combination of positive and negative characteristics, because his boys need to face the truth. Finally, his attention turns to Joseph, who by now is essentially serving as the prime minister of Egypt. His choices and counsel had preserved many people's lives during a terrible famine. However, Joseph's story has a sinister side, and everyone in the circle knows it. The question is, will they face it? Jacob says:

> Joseph is a fruitful bough,
> A fruitful bough by a spring;
> Its branches run over a wall.
> The archers *bitterly* attacked him,
> And shot at him and harassed him;
> But his bow remained firm,
> And his arms were agile,
> From the hands of the Mighty One of Jacob
> (From there is the Shepherd, the Stone of Israel),
> From the God of your father who helps you,

27

And by the Almighty who blesses you
With blessings of heaven above,
Blessings of the deep that lies beneath,
Blessings of the breasts and of the womb.
The blessings of your father
Have surpassed the blessings of my ancestors
Up to the utmost bound of the everlasting hills;
May they be on the head of Joseph,
And on the crown of the head of the one
distinguished among his brothers. (Gen. 49:22–26)

Can you say "awkward silence"? After all, who were the archers that bitterly attacked Joseph? Who shot at him and harassed him? We know. They did too. Joseph's own brothers hated him (Gen. 37:4), threw him in a pit (Gen. 37:24), and left him for dead. They had treated him in a way that was sour, brackish, like poisonous putrid bile from the gall bladder.

Please don't miss the all-important distinction. Nowhere in Scripture do we have any indication that Joseph was in any way a sinfully bitter man. However, without a doubt, he faced bitter circumstances. His own brothers were like archers who shot bitter arrows at him. Their own father said as much, even on his deathbed.

PULL OVER AND PARK

Do you have people in your life who have treated you in bitter ways in the past? Is that happening in the present? Make a list of events and people that come to mind. Is the solution to hum a happy tune and act as if such occasions never occurred? Maybe Jacob was on to something here. Perhaps the best way to avoid sinful bitterness of heart and life is to face painful circumstances head-on.

Harsh Treatment

Now fast-forward the story to after the death not just of Jacob but also of Joseph. Scripture tells us that after the children of Israel had endured several hundred years of severe bondage in Egypt, a new king arose in that land who did not know of Joseph. You may remember what the Bible records about that sad period of history: "The Egyptians compelled the sons of Israel to labor rigorously; and they made their lives *bitter* with hard labor in mortar and bricks and at all kinds of labor in the field, all their labors which they rigorously imposed on them" (Exod. 1:13–14).

Following the grammar of this passage is very important. "They made their lives bitter." This is similar to what we saw in Genesis 49. Bitterness is not something they first did—it is something they first experienced. Ignoring that reality is not an antidote to sinful bitterness of heart and life. It is an accelerant. That's one of the reasons the Lord recorded such sad and shocking events in his Word.

It is instructive that this particular use of the word "bitter" occurs in what we would think of today as the workplace. Do you need to pull your car over and park again? Your motivation for reading this book may be something that has occurred, or is occurring, at work. Have you faced bitter treatment on your job? Write out examples and people who come to mind. Before you judge such activity as unnecessary or unspiritual, ask yourself—is that not exactly what the Lord himself is doing in this passage?

This principle goes far beyond what we read in Exodus 1. Soon the Lord will perform a series of miracles that will become the bedrock of Israel's history and a powerful revelation of God's redemptive hand. After the first nine plagues on Egypt, the Lord issues a new set of instructions to Moses and Aaron. They are to tell the people to prepare an unblemished lamb and "take some of the blood and put it on the two doorposts and on the lintel of the houses in which they eat it" (Exod. 12:7). A few verses later God gives the awesome announcement:

> For I will go through the land of Egypt on that night, and will strike down all the firstborn in the land of Egypt, both man and beast; and against all the gods of Egypt I will execute judgments—I am the LORD. The blood shall be a sign for you on the houses where you live; and when I see the blood I will pass over you, and no plague will befall you to destroy you when I strike the land of Egypt. (Exod. 12:12–13)

Even before the events actually occur, God gives very specific instructions about a meal he wants His people to eat annually—the Passover—to commemorate what is about to unfold. Regarding the lamb, "They shall eat the flesh the same night, roasted with fire, and they shall eat it with unleavened bread and *bitter* herbs" (Exod. 12:8). The Lord never wanted his people to forget or ignore the bitter circumstances that attended their enslavement. Instead, he wanted them to face and even memorialize them.

These bitter herbs were a kind of lettuce or endive. Bible scholars give us two pieces of information that make the presence and focal point of these bitter herbs astounding. First, they are indigenous to Egypt.[2] This was Egyptian food. Wherever God took the Israelites in the wilderness wanderings and on into the promised land, he wanted his people to remember what it was like to live under the strong and relentless hand of their Egyptian oppressors. Second, the grammar suggests that the bitter herbs were not some sort of garnish but "the basis of the meal."[3] God's chosen people were to face, year after year, the bitter circumstances their evil captors placed upon them.

Imagine the explosion of tastes as worshipers ate that meal. Their mouths were filled with a dietary reminder of how hard the Egyptians had made their lives and the lives of their ancestors. Imagine taking a bite and thinking about how your father and grandfather suffered. Another bite as you contemplate what life must have been like for your mom and grandma, aunts and uncles. The Lord wanted generation after generation to consume food that caused their taste buds to recoil so they would long for something better.

Then came the odd and yet delicious taste of unleavened bread, baked that way because of how quickly the Lord's deliverance would come. The sensation is markedly different. Now at least there's some sense of relief, something to balance the bitterness of the herbs.

Finally, there was the marvelous taste of the perfect lamb. Close your eyes and picture the experience. Imagine the delight and satisfaction of such an amazing contrast. Then, as a Christian, think about the Lamb to whom all of this pointed. Could facing the bitterness of our reality make it more likely that we can and will delight in the sweetness of our Savior?

Incessant Mocking

Another example of this point occurs in a story that is both powerful and shocking. The book of 1 Samuel opens on the scene of a man named Elkanah who had two wives, Hannah and Peninnah (bad idea, by the way). Almost immediately, we are told, "Peninnah had children, but Hannah had no children" (1 Sam. 1:2). I know as a pastor that whenever I raise the subject of infertility, some of my listeners or readers will grimace with pain. If you're facing this difficulty right now in your life, I want you to know that I specifically prayed for persons in your situation as I penned these words. Even Hannah herself wept over her barrenness.

Next, we read the horrifying news that Hannah's agony was multiplied because Peninnah "would provoke her bitterly to irritate her, because the LORD had closed her womb" (1 Sam. 1:6). Now the point of this chapter—that bitterness in the Bible is not just a response but often a reality—is coming through in living Technicolor. Scripture is silent on exactly what Peninnah said, because that's not the purpose of the text. However, we can almost hear the words that were sour, brackish, like poisonous putrid bile from the gall bladder. That was Hannah's life, day after day after day.

Most of us know what it is like to be mocked or ridiculed in some way. Whoever said "sticks and stones may break my bones but names will never hurt me" was not telling the truth. We live in a cruel, sin-cursed world, and the words that some people say to us are sour, brackish, like poisonous, putrid bile from the gall bladder. For Hannah, as well as for you and me, bitterness is not first a response; it is first a reality.

A Natural Part of Living in a Sin-Cursed World

We have to be careful whenever quoting from one of Job's counselors, but Eliphaz was right when he said, "For man is born for trouble, as sparks fly upward" (Job 5:7). This is why the apostle Peter warned his readers, "Beloved, do not be surprised at the fiery ordeal among you, which comes upon you for your testing, as though some strange thing were happening to you" (1 Pet. 4:12).

You may not have brothers shooting bitter arrows at you, or a boss making your work environment bitter, or a rival bitterly mocking your infertility. However, it's probably a fairly short walk from those examples to something that is hard and painful in your life. Bitterness is not first a response—it is first a reality.

Navigate Wrong Extremes When Responding to Trials

We've already come a long way from our initial question about whether you have any bitterness in your life. I'm quite sure that you, along with everyone else who reads these words, will now answer yes. We all have examples from the past or present that fit under this heading: *bitter treatment by others where we had no sin or responsibility in the matter*. It will take us several chapters to work through the best and most biblical ways to respond to this reality. At this point, consider two of the most obvious and potentially damaging extremes.

Complaining and Grumbling

Complaining and grumbling is the wrong response that comes to mind quickest for most of us. Some of God's people are professional complainers. For example, right after the Israelites finished crossing the Red Sea, Scripture tells us:

> Moses led Israel from the Red Sea, and they went out into the wilderness of Shur; and they went three days in the wilderness and found no water. When they came to Marah, they could not drink the waters of Marah, for they were bitter; therefore it was named Marah. So the people grumbled at Moses, saying, "What shall we drink?" (Exod. 15:22–24)

Amazingly, they behaved in a similar fashion when ten of the twelve spies came back with an unfavorable report of the promised land:

> All the sons of Israel grumbled against Moses and Aaron; and the whole congregation said to them, "Would that we had died in the land of Egypt! Or would that we had died in this wilderness! Why is the LORD bringing us into this land, to fall by the sword? Our wives and our little ones will become plunder; would it not be better for us to return to Egypt?" (Num. 14:2–3)

God's people can be incredibly skilled at complaining. Perhaps that's why in the New Testament we are simply commanded:

> Do all things without grumbling or disputing; so that you will prove yourselves to be blameless and innocent, children of God above reproach in the midst of a crooked and perverse generation, among whom you appear as lights in the

world, holding fast the word of life, so that in the day of Christ I will have reason to glory because I did not run in vain nor toil in vain. (Phil. 2:14–16)

We all know that grumbling and complaining is a wrong extreme. I hope we're also convinced that taking this course will quickly and naturally lead to even more sinful expressions of bitterness in our hearts and lives. Going back to our clogged stream metaphor, complaining and grumbling is like already having a troublesome logjam and then adding more limbs and another layer of mud. Such a response simply makes a bad situation worse. However, is the only alternative following in the footsteps of Ephraim Cutler?

Suffering in Silence

We saw in chapter 1 that when Mr. Cutler's son Charles died unexpectedly while prospecting for gold in California, his daughter Julia quoted Psalm 39 to describe her father's response:

> He is very much bowed down under the stroke—still he murmurs not, the language of his heart seems to be, "I was dumb. I opened not my mouth, because thou God dids't it." Occasionally we hear a suppressed groan as he walks his room with clasped hands.[4]

It's true that Psalm 39:9 says, "I have become mute, I do not open my mouth, because it is You who have done it." However, the first verse of the psalm explains David's reasoning: "I said, 'I will guard my ways that I may not sin with my tongue; I will guard my mouth as with a muzzle while the wicked are in my presence'" (Ps. 39:1). David did not want those who did not know the Lord to misunderstand and possibly twist his words and justify all sorts of sinful behaviors.

However, does that mean David suffers in silence? Not at all. Taking that position would mean ignoring much of the rest of the psalm. For example, in the very next verse he says, "I was mute and silent, I refrained even from good, and my sorrow grew worse" (Ps. 39:2).

C. H. Spurgeon said of this verse:

Inward grief was made to work and ferment by want of vent. Utterance is the natural outlet for the heart's anguish, and silence is, therefore, both an aggravation of the evil and a barrier against its cure. . . . Silence is an awful thing for the sufferer. Mourner, tell your sorrow; do it first and most fully to God, but even to pour it out before some wise and godly friend is far from being wasted breath.[5]

In a similar way, John MacArthur observed, "His [i.e., David's] silence did not ease his pain; it seemed to make it all the worse."[6] Let those words sink deeply into your soul. There's no question that while grumbling and complaining will lead to sinful bitterness, so will ignoring the hurt, suffering in silence, or affixing a plastic smile to a broken heart. Bitterness is not first a reaction; it is first a reality—and you must face it well.

Let Bitter Circumstances Produce Sweet Fruit

The sequence of the Passover meal helps us in our quest for overcoming sinful bitterness of heart and life. Sometimes people shoot bitter arrows at us. Others purposely or inadvertently create hard circumstances where we work.

Occasionally we have to endure bitter mocking. There are days when Joseph, Hannah, and the children of Israel feel like close companions.

Maybe we should stop grumbling about bitter circumstances on the one hand and ignoring their presence on the other. Instead, we should sit down at the table the Lord has prepared and take a bite of bitter herbs. Then another, and another. Be honest about the presence of bitter events in your life. Let those sour, brackish, poisonous realities prepare your life and heart for something sweet.

The Sweetness of Knowing Christ

Earlier we saw how Peter encouraged his readers to expect trials and difficulties. In his second letter he tells them, "Therefore, brethren, be all the more diligent to make certain about His calling and choosing you; for as long as you practice these things, you will never stumble; for in this way the entrance into the eternal kingdom of our Lord and Savior Jesus Christ will be abundantly supplied to you" (2 Pet. 1:10–11). Being honest and open about the bitter aspects of this present life has a way of quickly bringing you to the end of yourself. That can be a very good thing if you will then admit your inability to handle life on your own and turn to Jesus Christ in repentance and faith. One of the marvelous impacts of this decision is that you can now "taste and see that the LORD is good; how blessed is the man who takes refuge in Him!" (Ps. 34:8).

The Sweetness of Self-Reflection

King David also asked the Lord, "Create in me a clean heart, O God, and renew a steadfast spirit within me" (Ps. 51:10).

The more I meditated personally on how bitterness is first a reality, the more I wondered—have I ever been a source of bitterness in someone else's life?

Joseph's brothers shot bitter attacks at him. Have I done that to others? The Egyptians made the lives of the Israelites bitter with hard labor. We have 175 employees and hundreds of ministry volunteers at Faith Church—have I ever made someone else's life bitter? Peninnah found a vulnerability in her rival Hannah and mocked her bitterly for it. Have I ever mocked someone else in order to make a joke or gain an advantage?

I found questions like this to be incredibly convicting. I have never understood a person who says, "I have no regrets." I always feel like responding with, "Really? Would you like some of mine?" Thankfully, we have verses like 1 John 1:9, "If we confess our sins, He is faithful and righteous to forgive us our sins and to cleanse us from all unrighteousness." This reminder of where bitterness starts should cause all of us to ask penetrating questions about the impact we're having on the people around us.

The Sweetness of Acknowledging God's Sovereignty

Earlier in this chapter, when we were studying the story of Hannah, did you notice how the Bible doesn't shy away from affirming God's role in Hannah's barrenness? "Her rival, however, would provoke her bitterly to irritate her, because the LORD had closed her womb" (1 Sam. 1:6). Hannah knew that, and what unfolds next is a marvelous display of faith. She prays so passionately to her sovereign God that Eli the priest confuses her devotion for intoxication. She explains, "I have drunk neither wine nor strong drink, but I have poured out my soul unto the LORD" (1 Sam. 1:15). She uses the context of her bitterness to find a new level of sweet trust in God's power.

C. H. Spurgeon reportedly told his church family, "I have learned to kiss the wave that throws me against the Rock of Ages."[7] Exactly.

Bitter circumstances can actually become the basis and accelerant for such devotion. The prophet Habakkuk sounded a similar refrain when he said:

> Though the fig tree should not blossom
> And there be no fruit on the vines,
> Though the yield of the olive should fail
> And the fields produce no food,
> Though the flock should be cut off from the fold
> And there be no cattle in the stalls,
> Yet I will exult in the LORD,
> I will rejoice in the God of my salvation.
>   (Hab. 3:17–18)

Hannah, Spurgeon, and Habakkuk experienced a new level of sweetness in their walk with God after tasting the bitterness of disappointing circumstances.

The Sweetness of Drinking from God's Word

"How sweet are Your words to my taste! Yes, sweeter than honey to my mouth" (Ps. 119:103). People who have walked with God for many years can often point to times when Scripture has been especially precious to them. When they describe the setting of their experience, it is almost always during a time of bitter circumstances that the sweetness of God's Word is especially evident.

The Sweetness of Longing for Our Eternal Home

Frequently as a pastor, I have the privilege and responsibility of ministering to people whose circumstances will probably not improve in this life. The bankrupt business is gone. The untreatable cancer isn't going away. The deceased spouse isn't coming home.

At such times, the bitterness of what they are facing is strong and pungent. We often find ourselves quoting together the amazing words of 1 Peter 1:6, "In this you greatly rejoice, even though now for a little while, if necessary, you have been distressed by various trials." How in the world could Peter use the phrase "little while" to describe bitter circumstances that some people will face the rest of their lives? It is because it is just for the rest of our lives here on earth.

We don't always think about the sweetness of heaven when things are going well. However, when our lives are filled with bitter herbs, our hope of heaven can and must be our sweet refuge.

Facing bitter circumstances is an important step in our journey. It requires courage and authenticity to acknowledge the painful aspects of living in this sin-cursed world. However, there's also a corresponding depth of relationship with Jesus available to all who will be honest about the struggle. Our next chapters will expand our understanding of both the problem and especially the solutions we find in the gospel. Hard roads can actually be good if they lead to delightful destinations.

» QUESTIONS FOR PERSONAL REFLECTION

1. Have you been conditioned by a watered-down "just be joyful" version of Christianity? How and in what ways? What does that look like in your life?

2. Whose experience in this chapter most resembles your own: Hannah, Joseph, or the children of Israel? Explain your answer.

3. What lessons can you take away from the fact that God wanted his children to prepare bitter herbs as the basis of their Passover meal?

» QUESTIONS FOR GROUP DISCUSSION

1. Which of the two wrong extremes highlighted in this chapter do you tend to fall into: sinful complaining or suffering in silence?

2. How did Jesus Christ perfectly fulfill the picture of the Passover lamb? In what ways do you find him especially sweet? How can the discipline of facing bitter circumstances make your delight in Christ even richer, deeper, and fuller?

3. How can and should a study of bitterness lead to self-reflection?

3

The Power of Bitter Lament

In 1987, just a few weeks after we arrived in Lafayette to begin serving at Faith Church, I had one of those experiences that taught me an enduring lesson about pastoral ministry. Faith's longtime senior pastor, Bill Goode, hired me with the plan that over time we would make a leadership transition, which eventually occurred eight years later. However, one of the first goals was for me to learn as much as I could from his many years of ministry experience.

On one of the first Wednesday nights we were in town, we were on our way to the church's evening prayer meeting and youth programs when I happened to look over at the car next to us. I observed a young married woman we had just recently met, but she was in the car with a man other than her husband. Now, I certainly didn't wake up that morning with the plan of sticking my nose in someone else's business. However, I was new at Faith and unsure of what Pastor Goode would want me to do with such information. So I thought, in submission to him, I should tell him what I observed and simply ask for clarification on what, if anything, he wanted me to do.

I should probably also add that at that point in my life, I didn't like confrontation. I tended to clam up when I was mad or upset. My pattern would have been simply to ignore situations like the one I had observed, but I thought I should start out on the right foot in my new job by at least raising the issue.

The next morning Pastor Goode and I were in the office reviewing several administrative matters when I casually mentioned what I saw the night before. Pastor Goode responded by saying, "We need to talk with them about that." I interpreted that to mean, "We should talk with them about that someday in the distant future, but not anytime soon, and in reality, probably not ever." I quickly learned that was not at all what Pastor Goode meant, because while he was speaking, he was also swiveling around in his chair and reaching for his hat. Then he put on his overcoat, which I interpreted as a sign that I should probably find mine. The next thing I knew, we were driving over to this young couple's house.

Pastor Goode was old-school when it came to visiting people, meaning in part that he didn't believe in calling ahead or making an appointment. He had an established relationship with this young couple, and he knew the woman's husband worked second shift, so they should both be home that morning. On the way to their house I was thinking, *I wish I hadn't brought this up. Steve, you need to learn to keep your mouth shut—this is not going to end well.* The next thing I knew, we were standing on the front porch and ringing the doorbell (*please don't be home . . . please don't be home*). Of

43

course, as Pastor Goode expected, they were home, and they invited us inside. We sat down and had about thirty seconds of pleasantries, at which point Pastor Goode looked over at me and said, "Now tell them what you just told me." It was one of those "maybe I should have been a dentist" kind of moments, but since I had no other choice, I told them.

What happened next was fascinating. The young couple actually started crying and then said, "Thank you so much for watching over our marriage. When you had a possible concern, you came to us right away and discussed it with us face-to-face." As it turned out, the husband did work second shift, and they only had one working car. The wife was driving with a cousin, and they had actually been on their way to attend the same church service I was.

As you can imagine, I felt very foolish at that moment (and I wish I could tell you that was the last time I have felt that way in ministry). However, I did learn an important ministry lesson that morning. *Don't let problems linger. Handle them right away with the goal of finding a biblical solution.*

Many of us would say that we don't like to do that. We prefer to ignore problems instead of facing them. We don't like the messiness that goes with confrontation and authenticity. Yet the apostle Paul told the church at Rome, "And concerning you, my brethren, I myself also am convinced that you yourselves are full of goodness, filled with all knowledge and able also to admonish one another" (Rom. 15:14). Pastor Goode was right—we should address problems right away.

This principle is much truer when it comes to our relationship with the Lord. Experiencing bitter circumstances hurts. Imagine what it felt like to be Joseph, the children of Israel, or precious Hannah. To them and to us, at the level of our souls these kinds of events feel and taste sour, brackish, like the poisonous putrid bile from the gall bladder. In that moment, regarding your relationship with the Lord, should you take Pastor Goode's direct approach to problem solving, or my tendency to ignore and avoid the issue? We can find the answer in a type of Scripture that we rarely discuss in many Christian circles. It is time to turn our attention to the power of biblical lament.

Introducing the Concept of Lament

Bible scholars believe that as many as one-third of the Psalms are laments. It is amazing to consider that such a significant percentage of Israel's worship hymnal is recorded in the minor key. Many other places in God's Word passionately express the laments of men and women who are walking through bitter circumstances. This is certainly the case with Jeremiah, the weeping prophet, who penned the book we know as Lamentations. A careful reading of Scripture reveals many examples of godly men and women acting more like Pastor Goode (*we need to talk about this*) than me (*I feel like ignoring this and hoping the problem goes away*).

Pastor Mark Vroegop has written a helpful book on this subject titled *Dark Clouds, Deep Mercy*. In it, he defines lament as "the honest cry of a hurting heart wrestling with the paradox of pain and the promise of God's goodness."[1] I found Pastor Mark's study to be beneficial for my own soul and for my ministry to those the Lord has placed around me. I strongly believe that learning to practice biblical lament is one of the keys to facing and properly handling bitter circumstances before crossing the line into one of the sinful expressions of bitterness.

PULL OVER AND PARK

I encourage you to put this book down and take out your Bible. If biblical lament is unfamiliar to you, begin by reading Psalms 10, 13, 22, and 77. These are important and powerful examples of what we're talking about in this chapter. As you read, ask yourself several questions:

- Do I ever talk to God like this? If not, why not?
- How much do I know about the power and process of expressing lament?
- Is it possible that one reason I sometimes cross the line into sinful expressions of bitterness is that I have not learned the art of practicing biblical lament?

Four Characteristics of Laments That Honor the Lord

Perhaps one reason many of us avoid this practice is that we liken it to sinful complaining, grumbling, or speaking to God in ways that are disrespectful and dishonoring. For example, we may think about the many times during Israel's wilderness wanderings when the people shamefully complained in ways that revealed their faithless, idolatrous, and thankless hearts. Or we may consider a person in our life today who seems to be constantly grumping about something. We don't want to fall into that ditch, and rightfully so. However, God has included this kind of material in his Word to guide us into an authentic relationship with him that only pain can fully produce. It is possible to express lament in a way that pleases and honors our Lord.

Addressed to Our God as an Expression of Truth

Biblical lament is a choice to speak directly to the Lord about our bitter circumstances. For example, in Psalm 13, David does not simply say, "How long?" as he thinks about his pain and misfortune. Instead he says, "How long, O LORD?" (Ps. 13:1). At this moment, he is a lot like Pastor Goode when I raised a possible concern those many years ago. Something is troubling David, so he metaphorically twirls around in his chair, finds his hat and topcoat, and marches off to have a conversation with God.

Some of us might view such an approach as being disrespectful and inappropriate. Author Todd Billings explains that the exact opposite is true: "It is precisely out of trust that God is sovereign that the psalmist repeatedly brings laments and petitions to the Lord. . . . If the psalmists had already decided the verdict—that God is indeed unfaithful—they would not continue to offer their complaint."[2]

In lament, we are saying to the Lord, "There's a gap between what I believe is true about you and what I'm experiencing right now. I don't understand it. I don't like it. I'm asking you for clarification." We see this same emphasis in the opening line of Psalm 10: "Why do You stand afar off, O LORD? Why do you hide Yourself in times of trouble?" (v. 1). In other words, "I *want* to talk to you about this, and I *need* to talk to you about this."

Such words can actually be an expression of faith and honor. When we lament properly, we affirm that God has the power and the compassion to provide the strength and answers we need in his time and within his will. To that end, David exclaims, "My voice rises to God, and I will cry aloud; my voice rises to God, and He will hear me. In the day of my trouble I sought the LORD; in the night my hand was stretched out without weariness; my soul refused to be comforted" (Ps. 77:1–2).

I wonder if for many of us this sounds like a foreign language. We know other people in the Bible spoke this way, but we never could. Is there a connection between that omission and the cultivation of sinful expressions of bitterness? Is it possible you're bitter about something in your life today and have spoken to all sorts of people about what occurred, but you've never addressed the issue with God?

We can find biblical laments in places other than the Psalms. Another fascinating example occurs at the beginning of the book of Habakkuk.

The oracle which Habakkuk the prophet saw.

How long, O LORD, will I call for help,
and You will not hear?
I cry out to You, "Violence!"
Yet You do not save.
Why do You make me see iniquity,
And cause *me* to look on wickedness?
Yes, destruction and violence are before me;
Strife exists and contention arises.
Therefore the law is ignored
And justice is never upheld.
For the wicked surround the righteous;
Therefore justice comes out perverted. (Hab. 1:1–4)

These words were spoken before Jerusalem fell to the Babylonians. Amazingly, Habakkuk is referring to God's own people. He doesn't understand why the Lord is allowing the children of Israel to behave so sinfully without judgment. So what does the prophet do? He goes directly to the Lord and utters a lament. I encourage you to read verses 1–4 out loud with the emotion and voice inflections that you believe Habakkuk would have used. This is not a dispassionate discourse from a mild-mannered observer of history. This prophet is fired up. He's upset. There's tension in his voice and disappointment in his words. He doesn't understand why God would allow this sinful behavior to continue, so he presents himself at the throne of God and begins his lament.

I appreciate the way one commentary explains this discourse:

> God is the friend of the honest doubter who dares to talk to God rather than about him. Prayer that includes an element of questioning God may be a means of increasing one's faith. Expressing doubts and crying out about unfair situations in the universe show one's trust in God and one's confidence that God should and does have an answer to humanity's insoluble problems.[3]

Exactly. This is why Mark Vroegop contends, "It takes faith to pray a lament."[4]

If you want to avoid or overcome sinful bitterness, learn to respond to bitter circumstances with biblical lament. Go early and often to the Lord, and speak honestly and openly about your questions and concerns.

Is it possible that your thinking on this particular point needs to change? This goes back to the story I mentioned about Ephraim Cutler. Cutler was a godly man who had a Christian influence in the early history of Ohio. However, when his eldest son unexpectedly died of cholera while searching for gold in California, Cutler would not talk about it to God or anyone else. Consider again what his daughter said in light of the biblical passages we have just studied: "He is very much bowed down under the stroke—still he murmurs not, the language of his heart seems to be, 'I was dumb. I opened not my mouth, because thou God dids't it.' Occasionally we hear a suppressed groan as he walks his room with clasped hands."[5] It would appear that when Mr. Cutler needed to be speaking to God the most, his incorrect theology on this particular point led him to choose to talk to God the least.

Portrayed with Heartfelt Concerns and Questions

In *Dark Clouds, Deep Mercy*, Mark Vroegop instructs readers who are facing painful trials to avoid what he calls both "the cliff and the cave."[6] His point is that sometimes a person experiencing painful circumstances stands on the cliff of unrestrained anger and screams obscenities at God in ways that are proud and accusatory. The attitude at that moment seems to be, "If I don't understand it, then it can't be understood" or "If it isn't working out in my experience the way I want it to right here, right now, then it can't be true." That's not biblical lament. However, neither is hiding in the cave and refusing to say anything to anyone at any time.

The biblical approach that helps us navigate between these two wrong extremes is choosing to be honest with God about what is troubling us. For example, consider the opening lines of Psalm 13.

- "How long, O Lord?" (13:1a)
- "Will You forget me forever?" (13:1b)

- "How long will You hide Your face from me?" (13:1c)
- "How long shall I take counsel in my soul, having sorrow in my heart all the day?" (13:2a)
- "How long will my enemy be exalted over me?" (13:2b)

Vroegop observes:

Once you start to see these questions in the Psalms, they jump off the page. These heartfelt questions have been in your Bible all along, but somehow they've been easy to miss. It is almost as if we don't understand the value of bringing our questions to God. Perhaps we think they're not allowed.[7]

He then references Michael Jinkins, in his book *In the House of the Lord*, who reminds us that God can handle our struggles:

"The psalms of lament open us to the greatness of a God who not only can hear, but also can handle our pain, our self-pity, our blame, and our fear, who can respond to our anger, our disillusionment in the midst of oppression and persecution, under the boot of tyranny and our sense of God-forsakenness in the face of life's most profound alienations and exiles." These psalms give us permission—even encouragement—to lay out our struggles, even if they are with God himself.[8]

I realize you may be saying, "I can't imagine myself speaking to the Lord like this." If that's where you find yourself as you process these ideas, I'm sure your hesitancy is well-intentioned, because you don't ever want to speak disrespectfully to the Lord. Allow me to respond in a purposefully provocative manner to attempt to adjust your thinking: *I thought you wanted to be like Jesus.*

Followers of Christ will instantly recognize that line of reasoning. One of our highest goals is to be conformed to the image of Christ (Rom. 8:28–29). When we ask ourselves "What would Jesus do?," it is far more than a slogan on a bracelet. We sincerely want to grow each and every day to become more like our Savior.

This is where Psalm 22 comes into the equation. This is not simply a psalm of lament but also a psalm that is clearly Messianic. Jesus Christ uttered laments to his Father while he was dying for our sin. At the holiest of moments, while the precious Lamb of God was shedding his perfect blood to atone for the sins of those who would repent and believe in him, he quoted Psalm 22:1, "My God, my God, why have You forsaken me?" (cf. Matt. 27:46; Mark 15:34).

PULL OVER AND PARK

Take out your Bible and slowly read Psalm 22. Listen to the words of lament. Feel the anguish. Admire the authenticity. Then turn to Matthew 27:33–56 and consider the crucifixion of Christ that occurred one thousand years after David penned Psalm 22. Think about the incredible mystery of God the Father turning his back on his own Son while Jesus bore the wrath and penalty of our sin. Then be amazed that at the moment of his most extreme pain and grief, our Savior demonstrated the place and power of lament. He quoted from Psalm 22—a psalm of lament. If it was right and necessary for *him*, surely it is right and necessary for *us*.

Filled with Bold Requests and Petitions

Biblical laments contain statements that may make many of us uncomfortable. However, remember that the writer of Hebrews instructs us,

> Since we have a great high priest who has passed through the heavens, Jesus the Son of God, let us hold fast our confession. For we do not have a high priest who cannot sympathize with our weaknesses, but One who has been tempted in all things as we are, yet without sin. Therefore let us draw near with confidence to the throne of grace, so that we may receive mercy and find grace to help in time of need. (Heb. 4:14–16)

I don't know what other word we could use but "bold" to describe what we read in biblical laments. For example, people call on God to arise and address injustice:

- "Arise, O LORD; save me, O my God!" (Ps. 3:7)
- "Arise, O LORD; O God, lift up Your hand. Do not forget the afflicted." (Ps. 10:12)
- "Consider and answer me, O LORD my God." (Ps. 13:3)

I don't know about you, but I'm not used to telling God to arise and do anything. However, verses like these are in the Bible for a reason. We also read prayers to help us understand what is occurring, as in Psalm 13:3, where David says, "Enlighten my eyes, or I will sleep the sleep of death." Those are words spoken authentically to God with an expression of how serious matters really are.

Biblical laments call on God to keep his promises. In Psalm 25:6, David tells the Lord, "Remember, O LORD, Your compassion and Your lovingkindnesses, for they have been from of old." What a fascinating thing to say to the God of heaven. When we model this aspect of biblical lament, we are not suggesting that God has forgotten, but instead we are asking him to close the gap between his statement of the promise and its fulfillment in our particular circumstances. This is a bold request to make to the Lord. However, speaking to him in this way honors his character and prevents us from becoming sinfully bitter.

At times, it is right and necessary to ask the Lord to perform justice on those who have abused and mistreated us. David says, "Fill their faces with dishonor, that they may seek Your name, O LORD. Let them be ashamed and dismayed forever, and let them be humiliated and perish. That they may know that You alone, whose name is the LORD, are the Most High over all the earth" (Ps. 83:16–18). Strong words, for sure, but there they are—right on the pages of our Bibles.

Biblical laments can even include a request that God vindicate us in his time. "Stir up Yourself, and awake to my right and to my cause, my God and my Lord. Judge me, O LORD my God, according to Your righteousness, and do not let them rejoice over me" (Ps. 35:23–24).

If we were to unpack your prayers over the past week, or month, or year, how many of them sound anything like the prayers of lament we are studying? Is it possible that some of us have set ourselves up for a bitter heart and life because we have not followed this biblical model of speaking authentically to the Lord?

Concluded with a Commitment to Trust and Praise

Biblical lament does not end in frustration and despair. Instead we find hope and trust because such prayer points our hearts toward the Lord's love, strength, and wisdom. C. H. Spurgeon once told his congregation,

> Would you lose your sorrow? Would you drown your cares? Then go, plunge yourself in the Godhead's deepest sea; be lost in his immensity; and you shall come forth as from a couch of rest, refreshed and invigorated. I know nothing which can so comfort the soul; so calm the swelling billows of sorrow and grief; so speak peace to the winds of trial, as a devout musing upon the subject of the Godhead.[9]

David says, "But I have trusted in Your lovingkindness; my heart shall rejoice in Your salvation. I will sing to the LORD, because He has dealt bountifully with me" (Ps. 13:5–6). The route to such confidence is often biblical lament.

We had a powerful example of this in our town when Purdue University student Tyler Trent was diagnosed with a form of incurable bone cancer. Tyler was a larger-than-life figure on Purdue's campus. He was known for dressing up in all sorts of outlandish costumes and cheering Purdue's sports teams to victory. Tyler was also a committed follower of Jesus Christ. The combination of his sincere faith and his joyful support of Purdue athletics provided a national platform to speak about the beauty of his Savior.

Tyler was also a member of the church where Mark Vroegop serves as pastor—College Park Church in Indianapolis. On the occasion of Tyler's death, Mark wrote a lament that went viral on the internet and is a marvelous example of how to use this important tool to avoid sinful bitterness. He wrote:

Oh Lord, we turn to you on this hard and painful day. We look to you, the author of life and the giver of grace, because our hearts are broken with grief. A young man, so full of life and joy, is gone.

We grieve the loss of Tyler.

How long, O Lord, must cancer steal our loved ones away? This evil disease doesn't fit with your goodness. It mars, destroys, and kills. We hate its presence in the world.

Lord, we prayed for healing. And your answer is hard to accept. We watched our friend and brother persevere. But twenty years doesn't seem long enough for Tyler. We'd rather have a different ending to this story. We long for the day when Osteosarcoma is no longer a part of our vocabulary or our prayers.

Yet we know that you have purposes beyond what we can see.

We witnessed glimpses of your plan in the meteoric rise of Tyler's story. We marveled at the favor and the kindness showered upon him through his journey. We rejoiced at the platform you gave him to share his faith.

And now, Lord, we ask you to bring comfort to Tyler's family. They've walked beside him through every step in this journey. They need your grace both now and in the months and years to come.

We pray for wisdom and creativity for those researching treatment for cancer. We ask that Tyler's donated tumor and the money raised might yield life-saving options for future cancer patients. Would you heal many from Tyler's death?

But even more, Jesus, we ask for your name to be lifted high through Tyler's life.

You were the bedrock of his strength. You were the one who captivated his heart and gave him hope as his physical strength declined. We pray that thousands—even millions—of people will be led to the kind of relationship that Tyler shared with you.

Lord, on this hard day we choose to trust you. We believe you have ordained eternal purposes that we can't see right now. We believe that you gave Tyler the grace he needed to persevere.

We believe that Jesus rose from the dead so that one day our tears will be wiped away—once and for all. Through our pain and questions, we rest our hope in the One who said, "I am the resurrection and the life. Whoever believes in me will live even though they die" (John 11:25).

We know this was the strength that made #tylerstrong. We saw it because Tyler lived it.[10]

Learning to properly lament will undoubtedly be a work in process for you. I know it is for me. However, I believe the Lord is honored if we seek to use his Word to guide us as we relate to him when times are hard. Trust God enough to cry out to him, and watch your relationship with him deepen and mature.

» QUESTIONS FOR PERSONAL REFLECTION

1. How are you responding to this discussion of bitter lament? Has this practice been part of your relationship with the Lord? Why or why not?

2. Do you agree with the premise that practicing biblical lament is one important way to avoid falling into sinful bitterness of heart or life? Explain your answer.

3. Write out your own personal lament to God based on a trial you're currently facing.

» QUESTIONS FOR GROUP DISCUSSION

1. How often have you heard or expressed biblical lament?

2. What can we learn from the fact that Jesus quoted a psalm of lament on the cross?

3. What is your response to the discussion about avoiding the cliff and the cave? Take time for each group member to share which extreme he or she leans toward and what steps can be taken to achieve a more biblical balance.

4

The Place of Bitter Tears

Recently our family was having dinner with friends when one of them began telling us about his experience playing high school football in the late 1970s. He explained how his coaches would not allow players to drink water during practice because they believed it was a sign of weakness. Two-a-day football practices in Indiana on sweltering hot August days can be brutal on an athlete's body. Coaches today would not think of withholding fluids from their team members. But apparently some people years ago thought drinking water was only for wimps.

Sometimes we even joke about how bizarre our bravado can become. Many people in my part of the country love former NFL quarterback Peyton Manning because of his great years with the Indianapolis Colts. He was a class act

Content for this chapter is developed from a message presented by Pastor Rob Green on June 23, 2019, at Faith Church in Lafayette, Indiana, and is used with his permission.

on and off the field and was known for devoting countless hours to watching game films, practicing relentlessly, and going through game-day preparation rituals that were exhausting to consider. Then he began making humorous television commercials featuring his dry wit and impeccable timing, usually poking fun at one of his own obsessions in the process. In one memorable scene, he is "coaching" a new barista who is trying to make specialty coffee drinks. The young man burns his arm when steam unexpectedly comes out of a port on the machine, and he then collapses on the floor. Peyton's feigned solution is a classic Indiana-ism: *just rub some dirt on it.*

Many of us, perhaps especially men, were raised with such beliefs. One of my earliest childhood memories was when my father and grandfather were building a shed behind our house. I was just a little fella, but of course I wanted to help. My grandfather saw me trying to lift a concrete block and instructed me, "Stevie, that's too heavy for you to carry. When you drop it on your foot, don't cry." Is there any question in your mind what happened next? Wow, did that hurt. And you'd better believe I did my very best to follow my grandfather's instructions.

You too may have grown up in a similar culture. *Real men don't drink water during football practice. Just rub some dirt on it. Don't cry when you're in pain.*

The questions I ask in this chapter are: Does that kind of false bravado work when it comes to pain of the soul? What does God want us to do when we feel hurt, disappointed, wounded, or broken?

One of the surprising answers in the Bible comes from the significant number of times the word "bitter" is used to describe our tears. In tandem with learning the art of biblical lament, which we studied in chapter 3, our Lord also invites us to discover the place of bitter tears.

PULL OVER AND PARK

I encourage you to use a physical or electronic concordance and review each time the phrase "bitter tears" occurs in the Word of God. Read the verses before and after to learn as much as possible about the context of each example. Ask the Holy Spirit to help you begin evaluating your own heart and life on this particular aspect of the Christian walk.

What do you believe about the subjects of suffering, grief, pain, and tears? How have these core beliefs affected the way you process trials large and small? Does your approach make it more or less likely that you will cross the line from the bitter circumstances we all face to sinful bitterness of heart and life?

The Importance of Developing Spiritual Candor

I'm not suggesting in this chapter that there is a direct relationship between overcoming sinful expressions of bitterness and the number of times a person physically cries. We each process our emotions differently, and the last thing this study needs is legalistic expectations. A better goal is developing what my friend and fellow biblical counselor Bob Kellemen calls spiritual candor, which he defines as "courageous truth-telling to myself about life in which I come face-to-face with the reality of my external and internal suffering. In candor,

61

I admit what is happening to me and I feel what is going on inside me."[1]

For those of us who struggle with emotional authenticity, we should consider the example of King David. Contemplate what he says in Psalm 6:

> I am weary with my sighing;
> Every night I make my bed swim,
> I dissolve my couch with my tears.
> My eye has wasted away with grief;
> It has become old because of all my adversaries.
>   (vv. 6–7)

That sounds a lot different from "big kids don't cry" and "just rub some dirt on it."

Should words like this cause us to conclude that David was just a big wimp? Or that he cried himself to sleep every night? Remember, this is the same man who killed the giant Goliath and cut off his head (1 Sam. 17:25–26, 30). Later he killed two hundred Philistines to earn the right to marry Saul's daughter (1 Sam. 18:25). Yeah, I think we would call him a pretty tough hombre. Yet by his own admission, at times he made his bed swim with tears.

Three Benefits of Processing Bitter Circumstances This Way

Why would the Lord make the topic of bitter tears such a significant emphasis in Scripture? Studying how this phrase is used in the Bible can help us avoid or overcome sinful bitterness.

Bitter Tears Can Motivate Us to Find Direction

The book of Esther tells the amazing story of a Jewish man named Mordecai and his cousin, Esther. Their joint heroism rescues God's chosen people from certain annihilation. In the early chapters of the book, the chief antagonist, Haman, a high-ranking Persian official, convinces the king that all the Jews in his country should be executed on the same day. Scripture tells us, "When Mordecai learned all that had been done, he tore his clothes, put on sackcloth and ashes, and went out into the midst of the city and wailed loudly and bitterly" (Esther 4:1).

Is that how a godly man behaves—and in public, no less? Apparently. Mordecai loves the Lord and his people too much to ignore the pain and heartache of this wicked abuse. Practicing spiritual candor, which may include shedding bitter tears, provides clarity and direction for what we should say and do next, even when the storm is raging.

By this time, Esther had been promoted to the position of queen. When she hears about Mordecai's behavior, she sends him a change of clothes, and then she summons her servant Hathach to find out what is happening. Mordecai "gave him a copy of the text of the edict which had been issued in Susa for their destruction, that he might show Esther and inform her, and to order her to go in to the king to implore his favor and to plead with him for her people" (Esther 4:8).

Esther sends Hathach with her reply, explaining to Mordecai that if she approaches the king in his inner court without first being summoned, she risks death. She further reports that the king has not called for her in thirty days.

This news places Mordecai in a difficult dilemma because of his love and concern for Esther. However, his bitter tears provide a kind of ethical focus and clarity that help him understand what is most important in that moment. He then speaks words that cut to the heart of the matter:

> Then Mordecai told them to reply to Esther, "Do not imagine that you in the king's palace can escape any more than all the Jews. For if you remain silent at this time, relief and deliverance will arise for the Jews from another place and you and your father's house will perish. And who knows whether you have not attained royalty for such a time as this?" (Esther 4:13–14)

Those words are not easy to say—and they are not easy to hear. However, they are true . . . painfully true. Practicing spiritual candor and weeping bitterly can help all of us determine the core issues of God's sovereign plan and purpose, even in the midst of our grief. Had Mordecai not wept bitterly, he may not have had the kind of moral clarity and focus necessary to communicate to Esther about her role in the preservation of God's chosen people.

The impact Mordecai's courageous admonition has on Queen Esther's heart is a beautiful sight to behold. She says,

> Go, assemble all the Jews who are found in Susa, and fast for me; do not eat or drink for three days, night or day. I and my maidens will also fast in the same way. And thus I will go in to the king, which is not according to the law; and if I perish, I perish. (Esther 4:16)

Imagine if Mordecai had not humbled himself in this way. What if he had not cried out to the Lord and acknowledged his pain openly before God's people? Perhaps he would not have realized the significance of the threat and therefore the crisis that had to be faced. He could trust the Lord and ask Esther to risk everything because his bitter tears helped him clarify what had to be done.

The principle is clear: *bitter tears kept Mordecai from developing a bitter heart and life.* He could have sat in silent resignation and waited for the slaughter to occur. He could have developed a seething anger and disappointment toward God, who appeared to be abandoning his covenant loyalty to the people he had chosen. Or worse, he could have been like the recipients of the book of Hebrews centuries later, who were even tempted to walk away from the things of God because the circumstances were not working out the way they hoped.

On the other hand, Mordecai could have acted as if the news was not that bad. *Just rub some dirt on it. It's not my problem. Big kids don't cry. I don't want to endanger Esther.* Thankfully, this courageous man avoided both extremes by crying bitter tears, which motivated him to find direction for what the Lord wanted him and Esther to do.

PULL OVER AND PARK

What difficulties are you facing right now? Take time to write out two or three circumstances that are upsetting you the most from either your past, your present, or your anticipated future. What would practicing spiritual candor look, sound, and feel like in each of these situations? Whether literally or figuratively, is it time to shed bitter tears about what is occurring? As the pain of what is occurring comes into clearer focus, ask the Lord to give you direction about what you should say and do next because of a fresh realization of the grief and injustice you're facing.

Bitter Tears Can Motivate Us to Admit Wrong and Prepare to Move Forward

On the night of his betrayal, Jesus had sobering news for his disciples as they were leaving the Last Supper. Matthew explains,

> Then Jesus said to them, "You will all fall away because of Me this night, for it is written, 'I will strike down the shepherd, and the sheep of the flock shall be scattered.' But after I have been raised, I will go ahead of you to Galilee." But Peter said to Him, "Even though all may fall away because of You, I will never fall away." Jesus said to him, "Truly I say to you that this very night, before a rooster crows, you will deny Me three times." Peter said to Him, "Even if I have to die with You, I will not deny You." All the disciples said the same thing too. (Matt. 26:31–35)

The subsequent events unfold in rapid-fire succession as Peter proves he is completely unprepared for the challenges ahead. As prophesied, Judas betrays the Lord with a kiss, and as the soldiers come to arrest Christ, Peter cuts off the ear of the high priest's servant (John 18:10). Jesus rebukes Peter for his uncontrolled anger (Matt. 26:52–54), then turns his attention to the injured soldier and tenderly "touched his ear and healed him" (Luke 22:51).

Peter then follows the procession "at a distance" (Matt. 26:58) to see what will happen to the Lord. He must have been appalled as he watched the initial mocking, beatings, and torture. Matthew then explains how Jesus's prophecy to Peter came true:

> Now Peter was sitting outside in the courtyard, and a servant-girl came to him and said, "You too were with Jesus the Galilean." But he denied it before them all, saying, "I do not know what you are talking about." When he had gone out to the gateway, another servant-girl saw him and said to those who were there, "This man was with Jesus of Nazareth." And again he denied it with an oath, "I do not know the man." A little later the bystanders came up and said to Peter, "Surely you too are one of them; for even the way you talk gives you away." Then he began to curse and swear, "I do not know the man!" And immediately a rooster crowed. (Matt. 26:69–74)

There are all sorts of ways that Peter could have responded at that moment. He could have ignored the pain that was caused by his guilt and hoped no one ever found out what he had done. He could have blamed his failures on the Lord, or the Jewish leaders, or his overwhelming circumstances. But instead Scripture tells us, "And Peter remembered the word which Jesus had said, 'Before a rooster crows, you will deny Me three times.' And he went out and wept *bitterly*" (Matt. 26:75).

This was the beginning of a turning point in Peter's life and subsequent ministry. The juxtaposition of his failure and the substitutionary death of Christ could not be more stark and powerful. Peter's bitter tears of remorse helped him face his weakness and sin in a way that prepared him for repentance, confession, and forgiveness.

Thankfully, God does not leave his children in that position for long. Solomon proclaims, "He who conceals his transgressions will not prosper, but he who confesses and forsakes them will find compassion" (Prov. 28:13).

In Peter's case, Jesus metaphorically wiped his bitter tears away not long after the resurrection. Several of the disciples went fishing, and after toiling all night, they had not caught a single fish. As the sun was coming up, a man on the beach confirmed their lack of success and then suggested they cast their net on the other side of the boat. You can imagine these seasoned fishermen rolling their eyes at the landlubber's suggestion, but they followed his advice anyway. Imagine their shock when their net was so full they could not even haul it up to the boat.

At that moment, John realized the man was Jesus. Peter was so overwhelmed that he jumped into the water and began swimming for shore. You have to smile as you read the passage and picture the other disciples trying to navigate their boat the short distance to the beach while dragging a net that was "full of large fish, a hundred and fifty-three" (John 21:11).

They then gathered around the resurrected Lord, who had already started a fire and was cooking fish and baking bread for them. I realize that some readers may not like the thought of that particular menu so early in the morning. However, I'm sure that since Jesus was wearing the chef's hat, it would have been the best breakfast ever.

Next, Jesus deals with the man who had wept those bitter tears. Guilt is productive only if it leads to confession and repentance. The Lord asks Peter, "Do you love me more than these?" (John 21:15). Peter responds tentatively and humbly with a word for love that in the original language is far less intense. The pride and brazenness are gone as Peter peers into the tender eyes of the risen Lord. The bitter tears have done their work.

Then Jesus does something that only a merciful Savior would do. He asks the same question two more times to mirror the number of Peter's denials. In front of the other disciples, Jesus then repeats slightly different versions of the same basic point—feed my lambs. In other words, *Yes, you failed terribly, just as I predicted. However, now that your bitter tears have brought you to a place of genuine repentance, there's an important role for you in the accomplishment of my plan.*

As a pastor and biblical counselor, I have spent literally thousands of hours talking to people from our church and community about some of the hardest difficulties they have ever faced. Yes, there are times when people were horribly abused in the past and bore little if any responsibility for what occurred. Thankfully, God's Word has a rich theology of suffering to guide them through their pain.

However, the typical pattern is of people who were not only sinned against but who also sinned themselves either before, during, or after the event. Many are now extremely bitter and have often spent the majority of their time thinking and talking about the shortcomings of the other person. Scripture has a process for addressing that aspect of the equation at the proper time as well. But if you sinned in some way, it may be time for you to shed bitter tears as you honestly face your part of the equation. The cleansing impact of repentance and confession often has a dramatic impact on bitterness. The more time and energy you spend focusing on the marvelous grace Christ has extended to you, the less time and energy you will have left to dwell on the pain and hurts of others.

PULL OVER AND PARK

One of the hardest things for any of us to do is admit that we were wrong. Blame-shifting is as old as the garden of Eden. I'm not suggesting you're the only person at fault in the situation you might be contemplating, because often when there's a breach in a relationship, there's plenty of sin to go around. However, Jesus was clear in the Sermon on the Mount that before we try to remove the speck from someone else's eye, we must remove the beam from our own (Matt. 7:3–5).

Bitter tears can help you do that. Contemplate the power and holiness of God, just as Peter did when he saw Jesus's miracle with the fish. Isolate your focus to the ways you failed in what you wanted, thought, said, and did. Then dive in the waters of repentance and swim for the shore of God's gracious forgiveness.

As you do, that cold water will wash the bitter tears away. Then imagine who you will find waiting on the shore. Your merciful High Priest. Your restoring Savior. The One with the scarred hands and the pierced side. Think about the meal of renewed fellowship he prepares for those who love him. Think about the renewed mission he offers. Because of the beauty and power of the gospel, bitter tears can lead you to a place of greater depth in your relationship with Jesus.

Bitter Tears Can Motivate Us to Remember That Only Our Future Will Be Fully Satisfying

One of the many delights I enjoy as a pastor is the privilege of studying various aspects of the Christmas story with our church family each December. So many of the details surrounding Christ's birth are awesome and joyous. The song of the angels. The amazement of the shepherds. The marvel of fulfilled prophecy. The simplicity of the manger.

However, bitter tears are also present in the story. I believe this may be true for at least two reasons. First, our Savior came to a world reeling under the effects of sin's curse. The perfect Lamb of God was born against a dark, grim backdrop of wickedness and shame. Second, each Christmas season brings a fresh batch of tears to church families like ours. Friends and loved ones have died, and for some it is their first Christmas without a parent, a spouse, or a close friend. Jobs have been lost or families severed. Even as I speak at our Christmas Eve candlelight services in dimly lit auditoriums at our campuses around our community, I can see flowing tears mixed with the delightful elements of the evening.

That was true on the first Christmas as well. Matthew tells us,

> When Herod saw that he had been tricked by the magi, he became very enraged, and sent and slew all the male children who were in Bethlehem and all its vicinity, from two years old and under, according to the time which he had determined from the magi. Then what had been spoken through Jeremiah the prophet was fulfilled:
>
> > A voice was heard in Ramah,
> > Weeping and great mourning,

Rachel weeping for her children;
And she refused to be comforted,
Because they were no more. (Matt. 2:16–18)

The passage Matthew quotes about that terrible day is Jeremiah 31:15, where the Lord says, "A voice is heard in Ramah, lamentation and bitter weeping. Rachel is weeping for her children; she refuses to be comforted for her children, because they are no more."

This is a fascinating passage of Scripture because there are three different occasions of grief wed together as only the Holy Spirit of God can do (cf. 2 Tim. 3:16–17). First is the context of Jeremiah 31. Bible students know this as the delightful passage where God promises to make a new covenant with his people. However, the setting is one of great heartache and despair. Commentator Craig Blomberg explains:

> Tucked into these wonderful promises is Jer. 31:15, the lone verse in this chapter that reflects the current grief surrounding the Assyrian and Babylonian exiles. Jewish mothers have watched their sons go off to battle, some to die and others to be carried away captive to distant lands. . . . Ramah was six miles north of Jerusalem; departing captives from Judah's capital had to go through it on the road to the lands of the northern invaders.[2]

Imagine these dear mothers "crying in bitter grief." Close your eyes. Listen to the sounds. Experience the depth of their emotion. Then face this hard reality—their sons are going off to war against a brutal enemy.

Second is the mention of Rachel. That hearkens back to hundreds of years before Jeremiah, when Jacob's wife Rachel died in childbirth. She named her second son Ben-oni, "son of sorrow," and was then buried near Ramah. Apparently her name and the location of her burial became shorthand for bitter tears.

Third is the treachery of jealous, wicked Herod. To eliminate any threat to his throne, he sent his soldiers to murder all the infant boys in the city of Bethlehem. How would a mother respond when her precious baby was torn from her arms and then put to death? With bitter, bitter tears.

However, God never gives evil the last word. Jeremiah 31 points to the future hope of the return of God's people after the Babylonian captivity:

Thus says the LORD,

> "Restrain your voice from weeping
> And your eyes from tears;
> For your work will be rewarded," declares the LORD,
> "And they will return from the land of the enemy.
> "There is hope for your future," declares the LORD,
> "And *your* children will return to their own
>   territory." (Jer. 31:16–17)

Bitter tears encourage us to long for the days when God will make all things right. Later in the chapter, against this backdrop of bitter tears, God makes one of the most important promises in the entire Bible, the new covenant:

> "Behold, days are coming," declares the LORD, "when I will make a new covenant with the house of Israel and with the house of Judah, not like the covenant which I made with their fathers in the day I took them by the hand to bring them out of the land of Egypt, My covenant which they broke,

although I was a husband to them," declares the LORD. "But this is the covenant which I will make with the house of Israel after those days," declares the LORD, "I will put My law within them and on their heart I will write it; and I will be their God, and they shall be My people." (Jer. 31:31–33)

This helps us understand the value and purpose of bitter tears. They motivate us to acknowledge the brokenness of our sin-cursed world and cause us to place our hope in the future the Lord has prepared for us. Followers of Jesus recognize these words, because each time we celebrate the Lord's table, we think about Jesus raising the cup of wine signifying his shed blood and then saying, "This cup is the new covenant in My blood; do this, as often as you drink it, in remembrance of Me" (1 Cor. 11:25). The bitterness of sin and grief and misery are overshadowed by the cleansing power of the precious blood of Christ.

Amazingly, this same Old Testament passage finds its fulfillment in Herod's wicked deed. However, an angel of the Lord warns Mary and Joseph, and the baby Messiah is rescued. The ultimate hope as we shed bitter tears is the salvation that comes through Christ's death and resurrection. We rejoice as we contemplate Revelation 21:4, which tells us that "He will wipe away every tear from their eyes; and there will no longer be any death; there will no longer be any mourning, or crying, or pain; the first things have passed away."

» QUESTIONS FOR PERSONAL REFLECTION

1. As you consider your past, were you raised to think about bitter tears as being appropriate and valuable? Explain your answer.

2. Of the three values of bitter tears discussed in this chapter, which one resonates most with you? Why?

3. Is it possible that you have crossed the line into sinful expressions of heart and life because you have not practiced the biblical habit of shedding bitter tears?

» QUESTIONS FOR GROUP DISCUSSION

1. Share an example of false bravado you experienced growing up or one you see in today's culture that makes it more difficult for people to shed appropriate bitter tears.

2. Discuss other uses of the phrase "bitter tears" in the Bible, and brainstorm additional lessons together.

3. How can failing to shed bitter tears result in sinful bitterness of heart and life?

5

The Making of a Bitter Heart

We have all heard people talk about the proverbial "line in the sand." Those words probably call to mind multiple images for you. Perhaps you think of a gunslinger in an old Western who slowly moves the toe of his worn-out boot across the dusty street and warns the villain to come no farther. Or maybe you remember a politician or statesman using that phrase to describe the perceived limits of acceptable behavior for other countries. Whatever the context, the point is always the same—*you can go this far, but no farther.*

There's a real sense in which we have reached that point in our study of bitterness. Thus far, we have focused on the poison of bitter circumstances. God's Word is clear that this side of heaven, we will all face pain, abuses, disappointment, and trials. Joseph's brothers shot bitter arrows at him. The Egyptians placed the Israelites under bitter working conditions. Hannah's rival mocked her infertility with bitter insults.

It's important to make two crucial observations about such events. First, you and I are not necessarily responsible when people treat us this way. The Bible contains many stories of innocent people facing grinding affliction. Second, it's possible to respond to such treatment without becoming sinfully bitter. That's why the topics of bitter lament and bitter tears are so important. Where sin abounds, grace abounds even more (Rom. 5:20). Our merciful God stands ready to meet us in our time of need and guide us through trials in a way that glorifies his name and strengthens our faith. There is great hope in knowing that bitter circumstances don't have to make us sinfully bitter.

However, we have now come to the important point in our study where we honestly face how and when bitterness becomes sinful. This is the line in the sand that God instructs us not to cross. The good news is that the Lord is far different from the intimidating gunslinger or the threatening politician. He is our gracious King who stands ready with strength to help us avoid taking steps that would dishonor him and destroy us. Additionally, he is our merciful Savior who is willing to forgive and cleanse us when we have become sinfully bitter. The hope is that we don't cross the line into sinful bitterness, but if we do, he provides a way out.

The Centrality of Your Heart

Bitter words and actions are not like wax fruit we paste on the outside of our existence. If that were the case, we could simply address issues like bitterness behaviorally and keep right on moving. God's Word paints a much more comprehensive picture of how human life works. Our behavior, including bitterness, flows out of a fully functioning heart, or inner person. Jesus explained it like this:

> That which proceeds out of the man, that is what defiles the man. For from within, out of the heart of men, proceed the evil thoughts, fornications, thefts, murders, adulteries, deeds of coveting and wickedness, as well as deceit, sensuality, envy, slander, pride and foolishness. All these evil things proceed from within and defile the man. (Mark 7:20–23)

The word "heart" is used over seven hundred times in the Bible. It isn't simply the seat of our emotions or the physical organ in our body. In God's Word, "heart" encompasses every aspect of our inner person. It is our control center and includes everything about us that is not material. It is so important that King Solomon tells us, "Watch over your heart with all diligence, for from it flow the springs of life" (Prov. 4:23).

A Core Passage

Solomon also made the important observation that "the heart knows its own bitterness, and a stranger does not share its joy" (Prov. 14:10). This is why it's crucial for us to consider the core beliefs, habitual desires, and characteristic thought patterns that underlie bitter words and actions. Thankfully, the Holy Spirit stands ready to help us do just that. His Word is "living and active and sharper than any two-edged sword, and piercing as far as the division of soul and spirit, of both joints and marrow, and able to judge the thoughts and intentions of the heart. And there is no creature hidden from His sight, but all things are open and laid bare to the eyes of Him with whom we have to do" (Heb. 4:12–13).

Good News and Bad News?

Bitterness begins in the heart. I suppose we could look at this principle either positively or negatively. On the plus side, God has designed life so that we have the time and opportunity to address what is happening inside before those around us can see or are impacted by our outward behavior. I've always considered that a marvelous gift. I don't want to know everything that others think about me, and I certainly don't want others to know everything I think about them. We can also rejoice that as we apply gospel-saturated principles to what is happening inside, we can put a stop to what displeases God before negatively impacting others.

On the negative side, some of us are not as motivated to deal with our heart as we ought to be, because we have no external motivation to do so. Since no one else knows, there are no immediate consequences. Wise is the person who gives careful attention to the heart of bitterness and then addresses such issues before they grow into external behavioral choices.

Let's Meet a Bitter Man

This brings us to a man who could be considered the poster boy for bitterness. In the first book of the Bible, we read the sad tale of a man named Esau. He is one of the sons of the patriarch Isaac, and his story weaves its way through Genesis 25–36. We should note that the rest of the book of Genesis is devoted to the life of Esau's nephew, Joseph. They both faced bitter circumstances, but their responses could not have been more different.

Esau matters to our study for many reasons, including how the writer of Hebrews later uses him as a negative Old Testament case study. After an extended discussion of discipline, unbelief, and bitterness, he tells us, "See to it that no one comes short of the grace of God; that no root of bitterness springing up causes trouble, and by it many be defiled" (Heb. 12:15). Next we read these haunting words: "that there be no immoral or godless person like Esau, who sold his own birthright for a single meal. For you know that even afterwards, when he desired to inherit the blessing, he was rejected, for he found no place for repentance, though he sought for it with tears" (12:16–17).

Commentator John MacArthur suggests that "perhaps the saddest and most godless person in Scripture outside of Judas is Esau."[1] It's important for us to scour God's Word to learn everything we can about Esau's bitter heart *and then seek to avoid living like him.* The only thing worse than the tragic life of Esau is when we are on a similar path.

PULL OVER AND PARK

Take time to read the sections in Genesis 25–36 that touch on Esau's life. Begin formulating observations about this man's choices, especially from the perspective of the heart. What is God trying to tell you about this all-important subject?

The Challenge of Believing and Following an Unexpected God

Genesis 25 is the midpoint of this foundational book in God's Word. By now the Lord has made his covenant with Abraham, which becomes the framework through which we interpret the rest of Scripture. God tells Abraham that although he and his wife Sarah have been unable to conceive children, the Lord will make him into a great nation, give his people a land in which to dwell, and bless them so that they can be a blessing to other nations.

The fulfillment of these promises begins when "Sarah conceived and bore a son to Abraham in his old age, at the appointed time of which God had spoken to him. Abraham called the name of his son who was born to him, whom Sarah bore to him, Isaac. Then Abraham circumcised his son Isaac when he was eight days old, as God had commanded him. Now Abraham was one hundred years old when his son Isaac was born to him" (Gen. 21:2–5). Chapter by chapter, we learn that the God of the Bible is powerful, sovereign, merciful, and good.

Amazingly, God later tests Abraham by commanding him to take his only son, Isaac, and offer him as a burnt offering. Abraham's response is fascinating: "So Abraham rose early in the morning and saddled his donkey, and took two of his young men with him and Isaac his son; and he split wood for the burnt offering, and arose and went to the place of which God had told him" (Gen. 22:3). Imagine the faith necessary to behave like this. Young Isaac notices the presence of fire and wood, but then asks his father where the lamb is for an offering. In words that have especially amazed followers of

Jesus Christ, Abraham says, "God will provide for Himself the lamb for the burnt offering, my son" (Gen. 22:8). Then Abraham binds Isaac, places him on the altar, and stretches out his hand with the knife. At that point God stops Abraham and instead provides a ram trapped in a nearby thicket as a substitute for Isaac. Abraham names the place "the Lord will provide," and then the angel of the Lord reaffirms God's covenant through Abraham and his son Isaac.

Isaac has every reason to be a godly man. A few chapters later, through a process that only God's sovereign power could have orchestrated, God gives Isaac a wonderful bride named Rebekah, who comes from Abraham's own relatives instead of from the pagan Canaanites (Gen. 24). Rebekah's family even blesses her as she leaves them, speaking words reminiscent of the Abrahamic covenant: "May you, our sister, become thousands of ten thousands, and may your descendants possess the gate of those who hate them" (Gen. 24:60).

However, Isaac's faith was tested in a similar way to his father Abraham, because like Sarah, Rebekah also was unable to conceive children. Isaac prayed to the Lord, who answered by allowing Rebekah to conceive twins. Then the Bible tells us, "But the children struggled together within her; and she said, 'If it is so, why then am I this way?' So she went to inquire of the Lord" (Gen. 25:22). His response is astonishing: "The Lord said to her, 'Two nations are in your womb; and two peoples will be separated from your body; and one people shall be stronger than the other; and the older shall serve the younger'" (25:23).

Two principles are coming into clear focus for every person wishing to avoid or overcome bitterness. First, God delights in placing us in unusual, unexpected, and uncomfortable situations and then asking us to trust his Word, his character, and his plan. That was true of Abraham and Sarah and the birth and subsequent sacrifice of Isaac. It was true of Isaac and his marriage to Rebekah and the revelation about their twins. God is honored when we come to him in faith. Thousands of years later, Paul would explain to the Christians at Rome, "What then shall we say that Abraham, our forefather according to the flesh, has found? For if Abraham was justified by works, he has something to boast about, but not before God. For what does the Scripture say? 'Abraham believed God, and it was credited to him as righteousness'" (Rom. 4:1–3). It is equally true of people like you and me—God is honored when we trust and follow his plan by faith.

Second, often God's ways and plans are completely different from what we might have wanted or thought on our own. One-hundred-year-old people do not conceive children. A loving father does not sacrifice the very son who appeared to be the fulfillment of a promise. You do not find a wife by sending a servant back to your father's homeland, who then waits for a young woman willing to provide water for himself and his camels. The older twin does not serve the younger. As the Lord would later say through his prophet Isaiah, "'For My thoughts are not your thoughts, nor are your ways My ways,' declares the LORD. 'For as the heavens are higher than the earth, so are My ways higher than your ways and My thoughts than your thoughts'" (Isa. 55:8–9).

What does all this have to do with bitterness? You and I don't become bitter in our hearts when the Lord allows everything to go just the way we wanted or anticipated. Rather, in all those times, large and small, when his plans and instructions are vastly different from our own—that's when the sparks fly and the recesses of our hearts are exposed.

A Crack in the Covenant Line?

Isaac and Rebekah's babies are born just as God said. No surprise there, although the message becomes clearer as the story progresses that God has complete control, even over the order in which warring twins exit the womb. The oldest "came forth red, all over like a hairy garment" (Gen. 25:25). They name him Esau, and he grows up to be a skillful hunter and a man of the field. The younger is born holding onto his brother's heel. He is named Jacob and becomes "a peaceful man, living in tents" (25:27).

Then the writer of Genesis makes a stunning and prescient observation: "Now Isaac loved Esau, because he had a taste for game, but Rebekah loved Jacob" (25:28). Parental favoritism within God's chosen people? That didn't take long. And what are we to make of the cryptic statement that the reason Isaac favors the son who is not heir of the promise is because he "had a taste for game"? Surely Isaac would not ignore the revealed will of God because of some temporal physical craving? Or would he? And if that's the kind of shallow, temporal man he is, what might that characteristic look like in the life of his favorite son?

Focused on Immediate Gratification: "Red-Stuff Living"

We don't have to wait long for the sad answer to that question. In the very next scene, Esau comes in from the field and is famished. He points at the stew Jacob has made and says, "Please let me have a swallow of that red stuff there, for I am famished" (Gen. 25:30). Jacob, whose name means "trickster," is ready with a reply: "First sell me your birthright" (25:31).

Don't miss the significance of this choice. Red stuff or birthright? Immediate gratification or God's eternal purpose and plan?

This is the moment of truth. This is the line in the sand. The time for Esau's love for God to be tested. An opportunity for Esau to stand up like a godly man and value God's covenant blessings and provisions more than immediate satisfaction of his temporal cravings. Listen carefully to "immoral, godless" (Heb. 12:16) Esau's response: "Behold, I am about to die; so what use then is the birthright to me" (Gen. 25:32).

I call this "red-stuff living." I'll use this phrase throughout the rest of our study to describe seeking the immediate gratification of selfish desires and demands with whatever idolatrous resources are available at the time. Now we're getting to the heart of the matter. We do what we do because we want what we want. One way to watch over our heart with all diligence is to give careful attention at any given moment to the nature of our desires. We should be asking ourselves, *What am I wanting right now, and is this a desire God can bless?*

Scripture speaks about the centrality of our desires in many of its seminal passages about Christian growth. For example, in Ephesians 4:22–24, we are given the primary difference between the "saved lifestyle" and the "unsaved lifestyle." Paul explains in 4:22 that the old self is "being corrupted in accordance with the lusts of deceit." That's what was happening in Esau's heart on that fateful day. Paul's words should jolt us, because he tells us that our lusts are often deceitful and that they are "being corrupted" (present participle). Sometimes Christians think that after we come to faith in Jesus, we only have to deal with a sinful pond of residual habits that has to be drained. But the challenge is much more significant than that. We have the capacity to create and then act on new desires each day that take us away from joyful satisfaction in God and straight down the road that leads to sinful bitterness. *Red-stuff living is always just one desire away.*

Paul's alternative in Ephesians 4 is the new self, "which in the likeness of God has been created in righteousness and holiness of the truth" (4:24). We can choose in the power of Christ to crucify desires that displease God and replace them with desires that are consistent with the truth of God's Word.

If you want to avoid sinful bitterness, carefully guard what you want. This is the same point James makes when he says, "Each one is tempted when he is carried away and enticed by his own lust. Then when lust has conceived, it gives birth to sin; and when sin is accomplished, it brings forth death" (James 1:14–15).

Sinful bitterness in the heart always begins with misplaced desires. Often they come in the form of unreasonable expectations we set up for the people and situations around us. Our children, spouse, coworkers, neighbors, and everyone else must behave in a certain way. We must have a perfect house. The holiday meal has to be Hallmark-worthy. And on and on and on. Once we go from "I'd like to have" to "I must have," there's idolatry in the Crock-Pot of our heart. We demand that people treat us in a certain way. We seethe with anger when they don't meet our expectations. We pout, complain, and curse. And we begin searching for something—anything—that will immediately satisfy the craving. Give me a swallow of that red stuff.

PULL OVER AND PARK

Consider two or three situations where you find yourself struggling with sinful bitterness. Is it true that you often focus on the failures of the other people involved? What happens when you turn the microscope on your own heart?

Write out what you characteristically crave during those moments. It could be approval, escape, sexual gratification, revenge, or thousands of other possibilities. What's your "red stuff" that tempts you to seek immediate gratification, regardless of the cost?

Disinterested or Interested in God's Purposes: "Birthright Living"

The Genesis 25 narrative ends with these sobering words: "Thus Esau despised his birthright" (25:34). The writer of Hebrews echoes that same theme: "That there be no immoral or godless person like Esau, who sold his own birthright for a single meal" (Heb. 12:16).

You and I face choices like this every day. Red stuff or birthright? Immediate gratification or seeking God's purposes? Here is a typical example. This morning I decided to wake up early and drive to my office to work on this chapter.

I decided to reward this heroic effort, in advance, with a cup of coffee from one of my favorite restaurants. When I arrived, the line at the drive-through was unusually long, so I decided to walk in. Once inside, I saw the problem—the staff was training several new employees. I don't like waiting, especially when I'm trying to get to my office to do "God's work." The red-stuff temptation was right in my face. *I must have immediate service by fully attentive employees who appreciate my business* . . . and on and on. That idolatrous path leads to all sorts of bitter thoughts.

However, there's a better way. Let's call it "birthright living." We will use this phrase throughout the rest of our study to describe seeking to identify and pursue God's plans and purposes through his strength at whatever personal cost is necessary in the moment.

In this case, that means simple things. Silently praying for these new employees as they try to learn new skills. Smiling at the other customers and interacting in whatever way is appropriate. Looking for needs, opportunities, and missional moments. Thanking God for the beautiful day and the opportunity to learn patience—again.

When I finally reached the counter, the young lady looked at me and asked, "The usual?" I was surprised she recognized me, until I realized she often takes my drive-through order on Sunday mornings when I'm on my way to church. She knows I'm a pastor—I often kid her about putting extra caffeine in my brew because our church family likes especially long sermons. Had I grabbed for the red stuff while I waited in line, I may have blown my testimony with this woman, who knows very well that I claim to be a follower of Jesus.

PULL OVER AND PARK

As a follower of Christ, how would you describe your birthright? Write out words that define your identity in Christ. If this is a new concept for you, begin in places like Ephesians 1, and note the words that are used to explain your position as a redeemed child of God. Next, write out the promises you enjoy in Jesus. Esau was rejecting the covenant promises made to his father and grandfather—what promises have you received in God's Word? Then discuss the purposes for which God saved you. Consider verses like Romans 8:28–29 and 2 Corinthians 5:9 and the concepts of pleasing God and becoming more like Christ. Study 2 Corinthians 5:17–21 and John 15:16 about your role as a fruitful ambassador.

This is a robust topic in God's Word, and there are hundreds of verses that help us understand our birthright. Every time you reach for your birthright and ignore the red stuff, you will find joy in achieving the purposes God has for you in that moment (John 13:17). Sometimes it is as simple as waiting patiently in line for your coffee.

Cultivating Dishonest Narratives

Fast-forward the Genesis story to chapter 27. Isaac is on his deathbed. In ancient times, that was when a patriarch would pronounce blessings on his descendants. Strangely, Isaac turns to his older son, Esau. Surely he isn't going to go against the clear plan that the angel of the Lord had revealed prior to his sons' birth about the older serving the younger, is he?

What would possibly motivate Isaac to reject God's covenant plan? Red stuff. Call this "like father, like son, like father." Remember from Genesis 25 that Isaac favored Esau because Isaac "had a taste for game" (25:30). He was a precursor to the false teachers in Paul's day whose god was their belly (Phil. 3:19).

Isaac's wife, Rebekah, steps in and concocts a plan for Jacob to dress up like Esau while she cooks a batch of savory stew. Jacob then fools his weak-eyed father, who subsequently pronounces the blessing that should have been given to Jacob in the first place.

The camera then pans over to Esau, who comes in with yet another batch of red stuff. Are you sick of it yet? God wants you to be. Esau presents it to Isaac, who realizes the deception and announces it to his dejected son. Don't miss the next words in the text: "When Esau heard the words of his father, he cried out with an exceedingly great and bitter cry" (Gen. 27:34). Not just any cry—a *bitter* cry. Christians who believe in verbal, plenary inspiration believe *every* word of Scripture was put there by God for a specific reason (2 Tim. 3:16–17). Esau had been cooking this batch of bitterness ever since he sold his birthright.

What Esau says next is crucial to our understanding of bitterness. "Is he not rightly named Jacob, for he has supplanted me these two times? He took away my birthright, and behold, now he has taken away my blessing" (Gen. 27:36). Jacob didn't *take* Esau's birthright. Esau *sold* it. This brings us to a crucial point about bitterness in the heart. Each time we review the disappointment and failure of someone else in the past, the temptation is to paint them a bit worse and ourselves a bit better. This is why Paul emphasizes in Ephesians 4 that our lusts can be deceptive.

Planning Spiteful Revenge

What happens if these ingredients continue to simmer in the Crock-Pot of a bitter heart? What brews when you mix disappointments, hurts, frustrations, and abuses with unreasonable expectations, inordinate desires, idolatry, and falsehoods? Esau's story answers that question. "So Esau bore a grudge against Jacob because of the blessing with which his father had blessed him; and Esau said to himself, 'The days of mourning for my father are near; then I will kill my brother Jacob'" (Gen. 27:41). That exactly matches what James says will happen: "Then when lust has conceived, it gives birth to sin; and when sin is accomplished, it brings forth death" (James 1:15).

The Hope for a Bitter Heart

Stories like Esau's can be convicting. If we're being honest, we'd admit that we all struggle with bitterness in our heart. Life hurts, and in those moments of pain and disappointment, it's easy to reach for the red stuff, even if it means turning our back on the birthright of seizing God's purposes.

However, followers of Jesus Christ can choose to reject Esau's example. We have been "raised up with Christ," and in his power we can "keep seeking the things above, where Christ is, seated at the right hand of God" (Col. 3:1). It is fascinating that when the adversary tempts Jesus in the wilderness (see Matt. 4:4–10), he does it with red stuff: "Turn these stones into bread." "Make a spectacle to draw attention to yourself." "Simply bow and worship me."

Each time Jesus chooses the birthright instead. He courageously embraces his Father's mission on that day and all the way to Calvary's cross. Just prior to his famous discussion of bitterness, the writer of Hebrews picks up on that thought when he instructs us to "[fix] our eyes on Jesus, the author and perfecter of faith, who for the joy set before Him endured the cross, despising the shame, and has sat down at the right hand of the throne of God" (Heb. 12:2). Reaching for another batch of red stuff results in a bitter heart. Embracing the birthright produces a Christlike heart of joy.

» QUESTIONS FOR PERSONAL REFLECTION

1. How much do you know about the biblical word "heart"? Would it be wise to study this word more thoroughly in the Bible? Do you give this area of your life the appropriate attention as you seek to live for the Lord, or do you place the bulk of your focus on external behavior?

2. What kind of red-stuff temptations are especially attractive to you? When you struggle with sinful bitterness of the heart, what desires start the fire?

3. What thoughts and Bible verses come to mind when you think of your birthright? How do you keep that a focal point of each moment in the day? What would less red-stuff living and more birthright living look like for you?

» QUESTIONS FOR GROUP DISCUSSION

1. Brainstorm the kind of immediate gratification temptations that we all face. Why is the desire for red stuff so powerful?

2. Who in your sphere of relationships is especially focused on birthright living? How does their love for Christ and their commitment to God's plan help them avoid sinful bitterness of the heart?

3. How significant is it that the temptations of Christ involved various helpings of red stuff? How marvelous is it that you and I do not have to have bitter hearts? What does this say about the power and majesty of our Savior?

6

Understanding and Embracing
Fatherly Discipline

One of my favorite books on American history is *Undaunted Courage* by Stephen Ambrose. It is a biography of the great explorer Meriwether Lewis and his partner, Captain William Clark. Lewis was commissioned by President Thomas Jefferson to assemble a team in the late 1700s to explore the lands west of St. Louis in search of a waterway to the Pacific Ocean. What an incredible adventure. The United States was only a couple decades old at that time, and few if any white people had ever seen the land beyond the Mississippi.

Of course, there were no maps. No one knew what to expect. The only way to know was to go explore it. So that's what this courageous team of soldiers did. History tells us that their expedition went fairly well at the beginning because there was an abundance of food. Because they were taking their boats upstream, the work was exhausting. However, the hunting was so good that the men ate an average of nine pounds of meat per day.[1] I have no idea how a person could do that, and perhaps there was some adventurer's exaggeration involved. But if you like to fish or hunt, imagine being in a place where, except for an occasional Indian hunting party, the land was entirely pristine. The point is that while the work was hard, they had plenty of food.

That is, until the second winter, the winter of 1805. The team was along the border between present-day Idaho and Montana, which even now remains largely uninhabited because it's so rugged and remote. The problem: there was no food. Even though they had expert hunters in their group, there was simply no game in the mountains.

Finally they met a group of Nez Perce Indians who were willing to trade with them. However, the only food the Indians had was roots they had dug up from the ground and dried fish, both of which the explorers excitedly purchased. The captains warned everybody about overeating, but that's a hard command to follow when you feel like you're starving. The men gorged themselves, and soon after, everyone become extremely sick. I will spare you the gory details that some of the men recorded in their diaries about that gastrointestinal disaster, but let's just say it was one of those "dying would have to be better than feeling this way" kind of experiences.

It turns out that the roots were extremely bitter. Ambrose goes on to explain:

> In short, for over a week the expedition resembled a hospital ward for the critically ill more than it did a platoon of fighting men. Herein lies one of the great stories of American history, even though it is a tale of what didn't happen rather

than what did. It would have been the work of a few moments only for the Nez Perce to kill the white men and take for themselves all the expedition's goods. Had the Indians done so, they would have come into possession of by far the biggest arsenal not just west of the Rocky Mountains but west of the Mississippi River, along with priceless kettles, axes, hatchets, beads, and other trade items in quantities greater than any of them would ever see in their lifetimes.[2]

Not surprisingly, that part of the United States is still called the Bitterroot Mountains. The moral of the story is clear: *be careful about what you put inside your body.*

That principle is even more important when it comes to bitterness of the heart. The words we have already quoted from the book of Hebrews bear repeating: "See to it that no one comes short of the grace of God; that no root of bitterness springing up causes trouble, and by it many be defiled" (Heb. 12:15). Those words occur in one of the most important passages in the Word of God regarding the subject of bitterness. It is crucial to understand that the context of this discussion is the issue of God's discipline of his children.

That brings us to the point of this chapter and a central thesis of this book. People don't become sinfully bitter when everything is going their way. It's easy to be happy on a holiday. Sinful bitterness occurs when we respond improperly to the hurts, frustrations, or disappointments of life. It can be defined as the seething and unresolved anger rooted in unbelief because the pains and disappointments of life were not processed through the lens of God's eternal plan and purposes. Allowing that to remain in your heart will have far more detrimental effects than those bitter roots the Lewis and Clark expedition ate.

It's true that we can't control how others treat us. And yes, we should practice biblical lament and shed (literally or metaphorically) bitter tears. However, there's often an Esau-like moment. Red stuff or birthright? Immediate gratification or long-term accomplishment of God's plan? In the broadest sense, those hurts and disappointments are part of God's fatherly discipline in your life. I'm not using the word "discipline" in a purely punitive sense, because in Scripture the word is much more robust. Regardless, you probably don't like discipline. I don't either—no one does. The writer of Hebrews says as much when he affirms in this same chapter that "all discipline for the moment seems not to be joyful, but sorrowful" (Heb. 12:11).

The purpose of this chapter is to change our view of discipline and position ourselves to process hard times in a way that embraces the purposes of God in the midst of the difficulty. A biblical understanding of God's discipline in our life is one of the most important keys to avoiding sinful bitterness.

The Bible Isn't Done with Esau

We could not do justice to the subject of bitterness without a thorough study of Hebrews 12. In this chapter the writer gives an extended discussion of God's discipline of his children and then uses immoral, godless Esau as the unfortunate capstone of a significant warning to the people of God. I'm aware that some Bible teachers believe this chapter is not really about bitterness but instead about apostasy or unbelief. I hope to show

97

in this chapter that the writer of Hebrews actually brings those three biblical principles together in a package that is essential for all God's people to understand. Rarely, if ever, do we find apostasy or unbelief without bitterness. And rarely, if ever, do we find bitterness without apostasy or unbelief. If those words sound shocking—good. That was my intent. The writer of Hebrews wanted to wake up his readers to where these tendencies would lead them, their families, and their church. The Lord may want to do the same with us today.

Important Background

To get the most out of Hebrews 12, we must quickly consider three other passages in addition to Genesis 25–27 and Proverbs 14:10, which we have already studied in the previous chapter. The original recipients of the book of Hebrews, who were Jewish, would have been very familiar with these seminal texts from the Old Testament.

A Sad Day of Complaining

We learned early in our study that the Old Testament word translated as "bitter" in our English Bibles is often the Hebrew word *marah*. For a Jewish person, *marah* was not just a word, it was a place. We have the same occurrence in our culture. When someone mentions Hiroshima, you don't just think of a city in Japan. You think about nuclear war. Or when someone speaks about the Twin Towers, the name calls up events far more graphic and significant than buildings in New York City.

The same is true for Marah. Exodus 15 tells the marvelous story of the song of Moses after the parting of the Red

Sea. It is a high point in the young history of God's people. However, that same chapter records that within days, "When they came to Marah, they could not drink the waters of Marah, for they were bitter; therefore it was named Marah. So the people grumbled at Moses, saying, 'What shall we drink?'" (Exod. 15:23–24). It appears that the bitterness in that location was not simply confined to the condition of the water. The people chose to grumble and complain instead of reverently trusting God for their provision. It was another red-stuff moment, and regrettably the people of God failed the test and revealed the depth of unbelief in their hearts.

A Habit among the People of God

This issue of unbelief and bitter complaining became characteristic of the Israelites. Numbers 14 tells how when God's people arrived at Kadesh Barnea, Moses sent twelve spies out to view the land the Lord was giving them. Amazingly, ten came back with "a bad report of the land" (Num. 13:32). By contrast, Caleb argued, "We should by all means go up and take possession of it, for we will surely overcome it" (Num. 13:30). That was a birthright moment if there ever was one. God promised them land as part of the Abrahamic covenant, and now it was time to act with courageous faith. Instead we read this sad account:

> Then all the congregation lifted up their voices and cried, and the people wept that night. All the sons of Israel grumbled against Moses and Aaron; and the whole congregation said to them, "Would that we had died in the land of Egypt! Or would that we had died in this wilderness! Why is the LORD bringing us into this land, to fall by the sword? Our wives and

our little ones will become plunder; would it not be better for us to return to Egypt?" So they said to one another, "Let us appoint a leader and return to Egypt." (Num. 14:1–4)

More bitter unbelief. Now they are threatening to apostatize—to renounce their faith in the reliability of Jehovah, the God of Israel. They sound like a nation of Esaus. We know the rest of this story all too well. An entire generation of men and women had to die in the wilderness because God's people reached for the red stuff instead of embracing their birthright.

Beware of a Bitter Root of Unbelief

Fast-forward the narrative nearly forty years. A whole generation of Israelites—all except Caleb, Joshua, and Moses—have died in the wilderness. Before Moses dies, he has the privilege and responsibility of preparing the next generation to enter the promised land. Imagine overseeing a forty-year funeral march to the incessant drumbeat of the importance in avoiding sinful, unbelieving, bitter complaint. At the beginning of the book of Deuteronomy, Moses rehearses for his listeners why their forefathers had been judged in the wilderness at Kadesh Barnea (Deut. 1:19–46). In Deuteronomy 29, Moses reminds God's people about the danger of the idolatry of the surrounding nations. He then utters words that will be used over a thousand years later by the writer of Hebrews:

So that there will not be among you a man or woman, or family or tribe, whose heart turns away today from the LORD our God, to go and serve the gods of those nations; that there will not be among you a root bearing poisonous fruit and wormwood. It shall be when he hears the words of this curse, that he will boast, saying, "I have peace though I walk in the stubbornness of my heart in order to destroy the watered land with the dry." The LORD shall never be willing to forgive him, but rather the anger of the LORD and His jealousy will burn against that man, and every curse which is written in this book will rest on him, and the LORD will blot out his name from under heaven. (Deut. 29:18–20; cf. Heb. 12:15)

Why would the children of Israel ever be tempted to serve other gods? The same reason Esau reached for the red stuff—immediate gratification of his idolatrous cravings instead of patient trust in the covenantal promises of God. The same reason the people at Kadesh Barnea complained and rebelled and threatened to go back to Egypt—immediate gratification of their idolatrous cravings instead of patient trust in the covenantal promises of God. Moses's point is clear: a person like that will be like a poisonous root that will have devastating effects on everything and everyone around.

God's Loving Discipline

Fast-forward the story once more, this time well over a thousand years. Now the promised Messiah has been given. Born of a virgin as prophesied in Isaiah 7:14, the Lamb of God performed miracles, patiently taught, and revealed the beauty and character of his heavenly Father. Then he died on the cross of Calvary as a substitutionary atonement for our sin and was raised the third day to prove that the price he paid was accepted by the Father. Next he began building his church (Matt. 16:13–23) of people who had repented of their sin and trusted him as Savior and Lord. The excitement of the gospel message was infectious and spread rapidly around the known world.

However, the newness began wearing off in some places. Persecution of the church grew. Life was hard and disappointing. Following Jesus was not always supplying the desired amount of red stuff, and bitterness began to set in. Therefore, a particular group of Jewish Christians—and in some cases, other Jewish people who had been exposed to the gospel and joined themselves to the church for social or familial reasons—were thinking about leaving the church and returning to the Jewish temple.

In his grace, God directed an unnamed author to pen the marvelous letter we know as the book of Hebrews. He speaks about the sufficiency and superiority of Jesus Christ, and warns his readers repeatedly and sternly about their temptation to apostatize. In Hebrews 11, he lists an entire group of men and women who remained faithful to God and his promises. Was there a lot of red stuff? Not always, but God rewarded their patient, obedient faith with a kind of joy that idolatrous, immediate gratification will never provide.

Next, the writer turns his attention to our Lord himself as a perfect picture of faithful birthright living that endures hardship and embraces the long-term promises of God:

Therefore, since we have so great a cloud of witnesses surrounding us, let us also lay aside every encumbrance and the sin which so easily entangles us, and let us run with endurance the race that is set before us, fixing our eyes on Jesus, the author and perfecter of faith, who for the joy set before Him endured the cross, despising the shame, and has sat down at the right hand of the throne of God. For consider Him who has endured such hostility by sinners against Himself, so that you will not grow weary and lose heart. (Heb. 12:1–3)

It is at this pivotal point in the book that the writer turns our attention to the subject of God's discipline. John MacArthur explains:

> The key word of 12:4–11 is *discipline*, used both as a noun and a verb. It is from the Greek *paideia*, which, in turn, comes from *pais* ("child") and denotes the training of a child. The word is a broad term, signifying whatever parents and teachers do to train, correct, cultivate, and educate children in order to help them develop and mature as they ought. It is used nine times in these eight verses.[3]

Why was this subject so important for the original recipients of this letter? They needed to change the way they were thinking about the difficult and disappointing circumstances in their lives. A biblical understanding of trials is crucial to avoiding sinful bitterness of heart and life. MacArthur goes on to explain:

> God uses hardship and affliction as a means of discipline, a means of training His children, of helping them mature in their spiritual lives. He has three specific purposes for His discipline: retribution, prevention, and education.
>
> We must realize that there is a great difference between God's discipline and His judgmental punishment. As Christians we often have to suffer painful consequences for our sins, but we will never experience God's judgment for them. This punishment Christ took completely on Himself in the crucifixion, and God does not exact double payment for any sin. Though we *deserve* God's wrathful punishment because

of our sin, we will never have to face it, because Jesus endured it for us. Neither God's love nor His justice would allow Him to require payment for what His Son has already paid in full. In discipline, God is not a judge but a Father (cf. Rom. 8:1).[4]

PULL OVER AND PARK

Take time to carefully read Hebrews 12:1–17. Is it possible that some of the people or events with whom you have become bitter fit under the heading of God's loving discipline in your life? That doesn't excuse the sinful behavior of someone else, but does it change the way you think about what happened? Has your focus made the cultivation of sinful bitterness on your part more or less likely?

Values of Fatherly Discipline

As mentioned above, we don't like discipline. That's why the writer of Hebrews tells us not to forget the exhortation found in Proverbs 3:11–12. We should never "regard lightly the discipline of the Lord" (Heb. 12:5). We should never consider it a commonplace thing or fail to benefit from it in the way God intends. If we want to avoid the root of bitterness from Hebrews 12:15, we must think about God's discipline in a way that is consistent with the teaching of Hebrews 12:6–14.

Proof of God's Love

"For those whom the Lord loves He disciplines" (Heb. 12:6). Read those words as many times as needed until they truly begin to sink into your heart and soul. Why does God not give us immediate and endless helpings of red stuff? The same reason parents don't give their children endless scoops of ice cream.

This principle has the potential to completely change the way we view events over which we could easily become bitter. Learning to remember that our loving heavenly Father is allowing this event for both his glory and our good helps us to ignore the red stuff and seek the birthright.

Demonstration of Our Sonship

I need God's discipline in my life to expose the potential idolatry in my often-wandering heart as quickly as possible. The fact that God is willing to provide the right balance of trials and blessings in my life is proof that I am one of his children. "If you are without discipline, of which all have become partakers, then you are illegitimate children and not sons" (Heb. 12:8).

My current office is in an urban community center our church recently built after being invited by the mayor to focus a portion of our ministry efforts in an area of town that has concentrated pockets of social need.[5] We love serving here, but it has a special series of challenges, including the fact that over 80 percent of the children around this campus are growing up in single-parent homes. While their mothers do the best they can, practically everyone would agree that families are more effective with the presence of a faithful, godly father. Our church is doing everything we can to support and serve these families, but the negative effects from the lack of a father who loves his children enough to discipline them are apparent in many ways.

I praise God that he has not left us in that position spiritually. Every time we choose to become sinfully bitter about something that is not going our way, we have forgotten the blessing of his fatherly discipline.

To Help Us Share in His Holiness

Our heavenly Father knows how harmful our red-stuff approach to living can be. Idolatry always overpromises and under-delivers. "He disciplines us for our good, so that we may share His holiness" (Heb. 12:10). I wonder how often we become sinfully bitter about events that our heavenly Father allows to help us become more like his Son.

To Produce the Peaceful Fruit of Righteousness

It is important to remember that after the Esau narrative, the rest of Genesis records the life of Esau's nephew Joseph. They both faced significant disappointment, but their responses could not have been more different. Joseph reached for the birthright and therefore became a godly, peaceable man who responded well to God's discipline in his life.

Living this way can help strengthen our weak hands and feeble knees (Heb. 12:12). It provides clear direction in painful times by making straight paths for our feet (12:13). If we feel battered, like a limb that is lame or out of joint, God's fatherly discipline can provide healing.

It is important to see the vital role peace plays in this discussion. "Pursue peace with all men, and the sanctification without which no one will see the Lord" (Heb. 12:14). This principle will come into clearer focus in chapter 8, where we study the issue of a bitter tongue from James 3. The bottom line is that bitter people will be in regular turmoil with themselves, with the Lord, and with the other people around them. If you let God's discipline have its intended effect, the resulting sanctification will make it far easier to live at peace with others.

Regular Motivation to Pursue God's Grace

All of us would say that responding wisely and well to episodes of God's fatherly discipline requires strength from outside ourselves. That's what this warning is all about. We are to see to it that we do not fall short of the grace of God. That means that if we respond properly during times of trial, we can find all the grace necessary to allow the discipline to have its intended impact.

Avoiding the Root of Bitterness

In Hebrews 12:15, the writer brings together the many strands we have been studying in this book thus far. Responding properly to God's discipline will prevent you from red-stuff living like Esau. It will prevent you from complaining like the children of Israel at Marah. It will prevent you from unbelief like at Kadesh Barnea. And it will prevent you from becoming the apostatizing root described in Deuteronomy 29.

The alternative is to be like the soldiers on Lewis and Clark's expedition. Bitterness in your heart will make you and everyone else around you deathly sick. You will cause trouble—lots and lots of trouble—and by it many will be defiled.

Godly Birthright Living

The beauty here is that we don't have to be like Esau. Instead of selling our birthright for a single meal, we can embrace God's eternal plan and purposes whatever the cost and the pain involved. When our hands become weak and our knees become feeble, we can "fix our eyes on Jesus, the author and perfecter of our faith" (Heb. 12:2). As we do so, we have God's promise that we will not "grow weary and lose heart" (12:3).

Regular, Genuine Repentance

Facing God's fatherly discipline will undoubtedly result in times of failure. Our creaturely weakness has a way of being exposed on a regular basis. Even in those times, we can reach for the birthright of quickly and honestly admitting our sin and humbly asking our Father to forgive us. There will always be a place for us when we repent like that.

Bitterness and Discipline Are Inexorably Linked

As I mentioned, I have had the privilege of pastoring and counseling people for many years. Most pastors will tell you that over time, we become especially convinced about certain biblical principles. Looking at sinful bitterness through the lens of God's fatherly discipline is one of those principles for me. So often sinful bitterness could be avoided if a person would choose to view their situation through the lens of the sanctifying purposes of our loving heavenly Father. "See to it that no one comes short of the grace of God; that no root of bitterness springing up causes trouble, and by it many be defiled" (Heb. 12:15).

» QUESTIONS FOR PERSONAL REFLECTION

1. How practiced are you at looking at the trials of life through the lens of God's fatherly discipline? What is your response to the material presented in this chapter?

2. Do you ever struggle with sinful expressions of bitterness because you have not considered God's purposes in discipline?

3. Regarding the person or situation with which you find yourself most bitter, how should the teaching of Hebrews 12 impact the way you think, speak, and act?

» QUESTIONS FOR GROUP DISCUSSION

1. What principle from Hebrews 12 did you find most helpful? Most hopeful? Most challenging?

2. What is the relationship between avoiding sinful expressions of bitterness and being at peace with God, yourself, and others? How have you seen this played out positively and negatively in your life?

3. Describe a person who sees to it that no root of bitterness is springing up in their heart and life.

7

Finding Freedom from a Bitter Life

In his groundbreaking book *Twelve Years a Slave*, Solomon Northrup tells the incredible story of being born an African American free man in Minerva, New York, in 1808, but then being kidnapped and sold as a slave in the Deep South just prior to our country's Civil War. Northrup's father, Mintus, had been a slave in Rhode Island, but he was freed when the family moved to New York. His son, Solomon, was therefore born a free man and grew up helping his family with farming chores, then worked as a raftsman in upstate New York. As a free man, he even started a company because of his ingenuity with rafts and had paid employees of his own.

Solomon eventually married, and he and his wife, Anne, had three children together. In addition to his work, he became well known in his community as an excellent fiddle player. In 1841, Solomon's wife took a job as a cook for a few weeks, and the plan was for her to take the children with her and soon return and reunite their family. While she was gone, a white community leader introduced Solomon to two men from out of town who offered to pay Solomon generous wages if he would join them and play his fiddle in a traveling musical show. They promised he would be back before his family returned and could surprise them with the excellent money he would earn.

Solomon agreed, but one night while they were together, the two men drugged him. When he awoke, he was in chains and on his way to being sold into slavery in Washington, DC. His story was later recorded firsthand by David Wilson, a white lawyer and legislator from New York. It is a sad and chilling tale of what it was like to be sold into slavery and to face the human misery and atrocities of that evil system. The problem was that once Solomon was relocated and enslaved in the Deep South, there was no way for him to get word to his family or acquaintances in the North about what had happened. Attempting to communicate or escape risked certain death, and Solomon actually witnessed fellow slaves being whipped and lynched for that very offense.

Twelve years later, a traveling carpenter named Bass came from Canada to construct a building for the plantation owner who had purchased Solomon. Eventually Bass learned about Solomon's plight and quietly promised to write letters on his behalf to contacts in New York. Bass finished the job, moved on, and months passed with no word from anyone. Then came the day when Solomon and the other slaves were working out in a field and a carriage pulled up with the local sheriff and a leader from New York who had come to set him free. The book was made into a movie, and this particular scene is especially moving. A man who had lost all hope is immediately and amazingly freed.

A year after Solomon's release, he and David Wilson wrote a book about his experience, and it sold over thirty thousand copies. That was eight years before the Civil War, making it not only one of the longest North American slave narratives ever recorded but also one of the best selling. Imagine the sensation of being freed from enslavement.

You Too Can Be Freed

As you read through this book, you too may feel enslaved to some aspect of sinful bitterness. It may be connected to a hurt or disappointment in the past, or to an episode of mistreatment in your life today. Perhaps you find yourself replaying the story of injustice over and over in your mind. You look for ways to avoid the person involved at any cost. The pain dampens your joy and enthusiasm for many areas of life. Perhaps you long for revenge, or you're envious because the abusive person seems to be prospering. When you look in the mirror, maybe you see a bitter face with creases of disappointment that run deep. You speak ill of that individual when the opportunity comes up. Bitterness is beginning to become an essential aspect of who you are. There's a low-grade, smoldering anger in your heart toward that person or event. It feels and sounds and tastes like the poisonous putrid bile from the gall bladder. The hard reality is that bitterness will enslave the person who does not fight it with the power of the gospel.

The great news is that we can be just like Solomon Northrup. We don't have to be trapped out in a hopeless field of damning and demoralizing bitterness. A redemptive carriage is pulling up, and our Lord and Savior is stepping down, holding out his nail-pierced hand, and extending his strong arm of redemption. Now it is time to think about how the gospel of Jesus Christ can free us from enslaving habits of bitterness.

PULL OVER AND PARK

Take some time to read Ephesians 1–4. Note especially what the passage tells us about the nature and power of the gospel. How does Paul describe our former life without Jesus Christ? What does he say occurs when a person makes a decision to repent and believe in Jesus? Write down all the words the apostle uses to describe our new identity in Christ, the gospel indicatives. Note carefully the specific process of change that is articulated beginning in 4:17.

Sit back and imagine—is it really possible to be freed from the power and penalty of sin? Especially be on the lookout for the subject of bitterness. If these chapters are speaking about Christian growth—the doctrine of progressive sanctification—do you think bitterness will make an appearance? What does Paul say about this enemy of our souls?

The Delightful Power of the Gospel

At its core, the gospel is the good news of the death, burial, and resurrection of Jesus Christ. His shed blood has the power to free us from the penalty and power of sin and reconcile us to a holy God. The righteousness of Christ is placed on our account, and our identity and potential are forever changed. In the book of Ephesians, the apostle Paul explains in glorious terms the impact this marvelous work of grace can have on people like you and me. We can be freed from the poisonous effects of sinful bitterness.

Facing the Significance of Your Enslavement

Paul uses powerful terms to describe our condition before we knew Christ. We were dead in our trespasses and sins (Eph. 2:1). We were walking "according to the course of this world, according to the prince of the power of the air, of the spirit that is now working in the sons of disobedience" (2:2). Imagine a person in that condition trying to address the challenge of a bitter heart and life. Verses like these call up images of a hopeless situation like Solomon Northrup's.

The story grows bleaker as we move further into the text. "We too all formerly lived in the lusts of our flesh, indulging the desires of the flesh and of the mind, and were by nature children of wrath, even as the rest" (2:3). No wonder bitterness can feel like such a deep and hopeless pit.

These same thoughts are sprinkled throughout Ephesians. We were in need of redemption and forgiveness (1:7). We were "dead in our transgressions" (2:5) and "separate from Christ, excluded from the commonwealth of Israel, and strangers to the covenants of promise, having no hope and without God in the world" (2:12). We walked in the futility of our minds and were darkened in our understanding, excluded from the life of God because of the ignorance that was in us and because of the hardness of our hearts (4:17–18).

These concepts begin to help us understand the depth of sin and its effect on the human condition. Bitter thoughts, words, and actions seem so powerful and enslaving because that's exactly what sin is. If this was the end of the story, our situation would be hopeless indeed.

Based on the Power of Our Savior

Paul also announces the incredible news that a Savior has come. Line after line throughout Ephesians reveals the beauty and majesty of the promised Messiah. He offers "redemption through His blood" and "the forgiveness of our trespasses," and all of this is "according to the riches of His grace" (Eph. 1:7).

It is possible for us to go from being dead in our trespasses and sins to being made "alive together with Christ" (2:5). This is what happens the moment a person repents and trusts Christ as Savior and Lord. The impact is so dramatic that we are even said to be united with Christ himself. Paul explains that God "raised us up with Him, and seated us with Him in the heavenly places in Christ Jesus, so that in the ages to come He might show the surpassing riches of His grace in kindness toward us in Christ Jesus" (2:6–7).

This can and should completely change the way we think about overcoming bitterness. I'm not advocating a legalistic or moralistic approach to living, where we pull ourselves up by our own spiritual bootstraps. I'm not saying we need to stop thinking bitter thoughts because the Bible says we should not think that way, or to stop speaking bitter words so that we can earn righteousness before God. A human-centered focus on growing and changing will never work. Instead, Paul is arguing for a gospel-saturated approach where we cooperate with the redemptive work the Lord Jesus Christ seeks to do in and through us.

For a Marvelous and Eternal Purpose

As if the story couldn't get any better, Paul also tells the Ephesians that God's redemptive plan in us was formed "before the foundation of the world" (Eph. 1:4). Stop and ponder that amazing fact. Overcoming bitterness is not simply a human goal that we might adopt on a random winter day. This process is part of God's eternal plan so that we could live "to the praise of the glory of His grace" (1:6). When people are learning to overcome bitterness, it isn't simply an exercise in self-improvement. We have the potential to think and speak and live in a way that puts the glory of God's redemptive grace on display so that we and others might praise him.

So That We Can Have Hope

Paul even prays that people like us would think this way. Sit back and ponder that for a moment. Consider the wealth of God's power. Take in the delicious aroma of his grace. Become a literal, personal answer to Paul's prayer:

> I pray that the eyes of your heart may be enlightened, so that you will know what is the hope of His calling, what are the riches of the glory of His inheritance in the saints, and what is the surpassing greatness of His power toward us who believe. These are in accordance with the working of the strength of His might which He brought about in Christ, when He raised Him from the dead and seated Him at His right hand in the heavenly places. (Eph. 1:18–20)

It's very important that you and I have genuine hope that we don't have to remain in the condition of sinful bitterness. We can have that confidence not because of the present condition of the person we see in the mirror but because of the eternal love of the Savior we see at God the Father's own right hand.

Key Principles for Change and Growth

It is now time to build a strategy for change and growth on the marvelous foundation of the gospel. It is fascinating that the subject of bitterness is given top billing at the end of Ephesians 4, as Paul lists specific ways we need to change. That should make us serious about change in this area, but also hopeful that the enslavement doesn't have to last.

Understanding an Essential Difference

The apostle becomes especially practical in the second half of Ephesians 4. Doctrinal truths like the ones we have been discussing are not given in a vacuum. God is most honored when his children make genuine, specific, concrete changes in and through his power. The principles in Ephesians 4:17–24 can go a long way toward helping us achieve that all-important purpose.

One crucial benefit of this passage is that we are given a contrast between the unbelieving lifestyle in verse 22 and the saved lifestyle in verse 24. The hinge on which this contrast turns is essential for understanding the nuts and bolts of how to change. Verse 22 speaks about an approach to life that is characterized as "being corrupted in accordance with the lusts of deceit." The opposite of this approach is to live "in the likeness of God" according to the "righteousness and holiness of the truth" (v. 24).

This means that spiritual growth requires a gospel-centered focus on living less by one's feelings and desires and more by the principles of God's eternal Word. What does this have to do with overcoming bitterness? Everything. When someone mistreats us, it hurts badly. Our emotions are frayed, and often our idolatrous desire is to hurt them back, cut them off, or make them pay. It takes us all the way back to the story of Esau and the temptation to grab another helping of red stuff in the form of thoughts, desires, words, or actions to alleviate the pain and even the score with whatever sinful means available in the moment.

What is the alternative? Running to the throne of grace to find mercy and grace in our time of need (Heb. 4:16). Choosing to be a visible representation of our invisible God ("likeness of God") and living by the principles of his Word ("righteousness and holiness of the truth"). Is this easy to do in the heat of the battle? Absolutely not. Never. But remember, living this way is not dependent on your strength and wisdom. The power of the gospel message is that you have been united to Christ for moments just like this.

PULL OVER AND PARK

Using the chart below, think through the last several events in which you've been tempted to become bitter. How many of your inner (heart) and outer (behavior) responses belong in the left column, and how many belong in the right? Seek to be as specific as possible regarding what you were wanting, thinking, saying, and doing. Then consider which path makes the cultivation of sinful bitterness more likely and which makes it less.

EVALUATING EPISODES WHEN I WAS TEMPTED
TO BE SINFULLY BITTER

Examples when I was feeling/desire oriented in either my heart or behavior (Eph. 4:22)	Examples when I was truth/principle oriented in either my heart or behavior (Eph. 4:24)
1.	1.
2.	2.
3.	3.
4.	4.

Learning a Critical Principle

These same verses give us specific information about how to change. Bible students refer to this as the "put off/put on" principle. In the original Greek, the words Paul uses are a clothing illustration. Just like a worker would take off their dirty clothes at the end of the day and replace them with clean ones, Christians grow by stopping what is wrong (in either their heart or behavior) and replacing sinful approaches with ones that please the Lord.

The beauty is that this happens both positionally and practically. In other words, the moment we trusted Christ, there was a put off/put on transaction. In the account books of heaven, we laid aside the old self (4:22) and put on the new self (4:24). That's why some Bible teachers, based on the tense of the original word, believe Paul is speaking in the past tense in this passage. At some point the argument is moot, because even if that is not his primary point, the argument of the previous chapters surely is that a put off/put on dynamic occurs positionally as soon as a person believes in Christ.

However, even if Paul is speaking in the past tense in verses 22–24, he is still clearly describing a present reality, because in the examples he gives in verse 25 about lying and verse 28 about stealing, the put off/put on dynamic is the operative way a person changes practically.

This is much more than just arcane theology. This approach is far different from the world's view that in order to change, you have to simply stop what is wrong. You don't stop lying by simply refusing to lie. The argument of verse 25 is that you also have to become a person who tells the truth. You must put off what is wrong and replace it with what is right. The same is the case with stealing in verse 28. You don't stop stealing by simply avoiding the wrong behavior. You have to begin working hard and giving to those in need. In the power of Christ, God's people stop doing what is wrong and start doing what is right.

Applying the Principle to Bitterness

Now we're really getting somewhere. If you lived in my neck of the woods, you would say that we're "cooking with grease." There are several different levels or aspects of sinful bitterness. For our purposes here, we'll consider core beliefs, desires, thoughts, actions, and words.

Our Core Beliefs

Our hearts contain key ideas about God, ourselves, those around us, and our circumstances. If our core beliefs are skewed, we are well on our way to sinful bitterness of heart and life. Remember Esau? He believed in his heart that his birthright was unimportant. He didn't love God or care about the accomplishment of God's plan and purposes in his life. We can never change until we give careful attention to what we believe. Solomon explains this principle in his description of a selfish person: "For as he thinks within himself, so he is" (Prov. 23:7).

In the areas where you struggle with sinful bitterness, what wrong beliefs need to be discarded and what correct beliefs need to be developed?

With regard to Esau, if we consider his story through the lens of the put off/put on principle, it might begin like this:

CHANGING SINFUL BITTERNESS

Put Off	Put On
Core Beliefs	Core Beliefs
God is not worthy of my trust or devotion. I'm justified in despising him and his plan for me.	God is good, merciful, and just. I want to love him and seek his eternal plan.
I'm the center of the universe, and my desires should reign supreme.	God created me to subdue the earth, including my own passions, to bring glory to his great name.

PULL OVER AND PARK

The example above shows how Esau might have completed the first section of the put off/put on chart regarding his core beliefs. Consider how you might complete a similar chart regarding the core beliefs you carry when you're tempted to become sinfully bitter, and be prepared to do so at the end of this chapter.

Our Desires

We want what we want because we believe what we believe. James explains the power of our desires when he writes, "But each one is tempted when he is carried away and enticed by his own lust. Then when lust has conceived, it gives birth to sin; and when sin is accomplished, it brings forth death" (James 1:14–15).

Is the Esau narrative making more sense? Because of his wrong core beliefs, he wanted immediate gratification. That desire became so strong that he thought he would die if he didn't get an immediate helping of red stuff.

We would do well to carefully examine what we typically want during times that lead to bitterness. The challenge is that we're often so focused on the sins of others, we fail to examine the sin that resides in our own heart.

Applying this principle can bring great hope and great relief. We can rarely change the choices of those around us. But in the power of Christ we can definitely change the nature of what we want in any given situation. Imagine if Esau had cultivated a heart that truly loved and honored God, so that when faced with temptation, he would choose to please and honor the Lord, even if it meant saying no to a temporal craving. His story would have been far different. I wonder how many of the times we have become bitter are because our own heart wants things that are idolatrous replacements for right desires that would point us to satisfaction and joy in our sufficient Savior.

CHANGING SINFUL BITTERNESS

Put Off	Put On
Core Beliefs	Core Beliefs
God is not worthy of my trust or devotion. I'm justified in despising him and his plan for me.	God is good, merciful, and just. I want to love him and seek his eternal plan.
I'm the center of the universe, and my desires should reign supreme.	God created me to subdue the earth, including my own passions, to bring glory to his great name.
Desires	Desires
I want immediate gratification to satisfy my longings.	I want to please and honor God, even if my temporal desires go unsatisfied.
I must have a God and people around me who give me everything I think I need and deserve right now.	I want to submit my desires to God's perfect will for myself and those around me.

Now we have added how Esau might have completed the second section of the put off/put on chart regarding the desires of his heart. Consider how you might complete a similar chart regarding the deep desires you often take into situations when you're tempted to become sinfully bitter, and be prepared to do so at the end of this chapter.

Our Patterns of Thinking

Remember how I suggested that we were cooking with grease? Now the grease is getting hotter, because we develop narratives that explain our stories. These are patterns of thinking we replay over and over. Whenever a new episode of disappointment or hurt occurs, it hits the skillet of our minds and is processed by these repetitive thoughts.

You know what is coming next. Consider Esau. We think what we think, because we want what we want, because we believe what we believe. Esau thought his brother stole his birthright. He told himself that version of the story so often that he probably believed it himself. To use the terminology of Hebrews 12:15, the root of bitterness that had sprung up became firmly implanted.

These ideas should have each of us shaking, at least somewhat, in our bitter boots. What if I have created a narrative about a particular person or event that contains lies? Is that not exactly what Paul says the unsaved lifestyle is like? It is characterized by futile thinking, darkened understanding, and deceitful lusts (Eph. 4:17–24). Here is a haunting question: *What if we have been justifying bitterness in our heart and life for an extended period of time, when the truth is that our thinking about what occurred contains false-hoods?* That's why Paul tells his readers to lay aside falsehood and instead speak truth with those around us (Eph. 4:25).

CHANGING SINFUL BITTERNESS

Put Off	Put On
Core Beliefs	Core Beliefs
God is not worthy of my trust or devotion. I'm justified in despising him and his plan for me.	God is good, merciful, and just. I want to love him and seek his eternal plan.
I'm the center of the universe, and my desires should reign supreme.	God created me to subdue the earth, including my own passions, to bring glory to his great name.

Put Off	Put On
Desires	Desires
I want immediate gratification to satisfy my longings.	I want to please and honor God, even if my temporal desires go unsatisfied.
I must have a God and people around me who give me everything I think I need and deserve right now.	I want to submit my desires to God's perfect will for myself and those around me.
Thoughts	Thoughts
My birthright is unimportant.	My role in accomplishing God's eternal plan is of supreme value to me.
The cravings of my heart are always valid and most important.	The cravings of my heart will often lead me astray if I don't test them against God's Word.

At this point the principles should be coming into clearer focus. Esau thought what he thought, because he wanted what he wanted, because he believed what he believed. What was Esau thinking as the red-stuff/birthright episode unfolded? The updated version of our chart presents one possible set of answers, along with what he should have been thinking instead. Consider how you might complete a similar chart regarding your habitual patterns of thinking when you're tempted to become sinfully bitter, and be prepared to do so at the end of this chapter.

Our Patterns of Speaking

Chapter 8 will be entirely devoted to the issue of a bitter tongue. It shouldn't surprise us that when we struggle with bitterness in our heart, invariably it will come out in the way we speak. That's why our speech plays a prominent role in Paul's discussion in Ephesians 4. "Let no unwholesome word proceed from your mouth, but only such a word as is good for edification according to the need of the moment, so that it will give grace to those who hear" (Eph. 4:29). Unwholesome words are best understood in light of the contrast Paul sets up in that verse. Unlike speech that edifies (builds up) and gives grace, unwholesome words tear down and destroy. How can we justify speaking such words? Because they are the natural outgrowth of a bitter heart. We speak the way we speak, because we think the way we think, because we want what we want, because we believe what we believe.

Consider Esau. He cried out with an "exceedingly great and bitter cry" (Gen. 27:34). He began speaking bitter lies to his father about what had occurred. Then he reserved some of his most bitter words . . . for himself. Do you realize that the bitterest person you may ever talk to is yourself? "Esau said to himself, 'The days of mourning for my father are near; then I will kill my brother Jacob'" (Gen. 27:41).

Thank the Lord for the hopeful alternative. Throughout the story of Esau's nephew Joseph, we find God giving the young patriarch strength to speak words of grace time after time, even in the midst of great suffering. You have the ability to put off bitter words and replace them with words that please and honor our sweet Savior.

CHANGING SINFUL BITTERNESS

Put Off	Put On
Core Beliefs	Core Beliefs
God is not worthy of my trust or devotion. I'm justified in despising him and his plan for me.	God is good, merciful, and just. I want to love him and seek his eternal plan.
I'm the center of the universe, and my desires should reign supreme.	God created me to subdue the earth, including my passions, to bring glory to his great name.

Put Off	Put On
Desires	**Desires**
I want immediate gratification to satisfy my longings.	I want to please and honor God, even if my temporal desires go unsatisfied.
I must have a God and people around me who give me everything I think I need and deserve right now.	I want to submit my desires to God's perfect will for myself and those around me.
Thoughts	**Thoughts**
My birthright is unimportant.	My role in accomplishing God's eternal plan is of supreme value to me.
The cravings of my heart are always valid and most important.	The cravings of my heart will often lead me astray if I don't test them against God's Word.
Words	**Words**
My brother stole my birthright.	I sold my birthright in a way that dishonored God.
I will make plans to kill my brother.	Murder is a violation of God's law, and I don't ever desire to sin in this way.

Esau's bitterness eventually impacted the way he spoke. The next installment of our chart demonstrates that sad progression. Consider bitter words you sometimes speak and possible alternatives that would be more pleasing to God.

Our Patterns of Behavior

Paul concludes his argument by firing a laser-guided missile at our behavior. That doesn't make him or us behaviorists— there has been plenty of emphasis on the heart in this chapter. However, God is powerful enough to help us change the behavioral choices we make every day. We do what we do and say what we say, because we think what we think, because we want what we want, because we believe what we believe. The gospel of Jesus Christ and the put off/put on principle can help us change every facet of that conceptualization to the praise of the glory of his grace.

Let all bitterness and wrath and anger and clamor and slander be put away from you, along with all malice. Be kind to one another, tender-hearted, forgiving each other, just as God in Christ also has forgiven you. (Eph. 4:31–32)

CHANGING SINFUL BITTERNESS

Put Off	Put On
Core Beliefs	Core Beliefs
God is not worthy of my trust or devotion. I'm justified in despising him and his plan for me.	God is good, merciful, and just. I want to love him and seek his eternal plan.
I'm the center of the universe, and my desires should reign supreme.	God created me to subdue the earth, including my own passions, to bring glory to his great name.
Desires	Desires
I want immediate gratification to satisfy my longings.	I want to please and honor God, even if my temporal desires go unsatisfied.
I must have a God and people around me who give me everything I think I need and deserve right now.	I want to submit my desires to God's perfect will for myself and those around me.
Thoughts	Thoughts
My birthright is unimportant.	My role in accomplishing God's eternal plan is of supreme value to me.
The cravings of my heart are always valid and most important.	The cravings of my heart will often lead me astray if I don't test them against God's Word.
Words	Words
My brother stole my birthright.	I sold my birthright in a way that dishonored God.
I will make plans to kill my brother.	Murder is a violation of God's law, and I don't ever desire to sin in this way.
Behavior	Behavior
He cried out with an exceedingly great and bitter cry.	He humbly acknowledged his fault in the matter.
He found no place for repentance, though he sought it with tears.	He repented genuinely and found forgiveness and grace.

Unrestrained sinful bitterness always results in behavior that dishonors God and harms others. Esau is a sad and profound example of this principle. The final version of our chart shows where the bitterness trail ends. Is there any bitter behavior in your life?

» QUESTIONS FOR PERSONAL REFLECTION

1. Have you felt trapped and enslaved in bitterness? When and in what ways?

2. Are you sure there has been a definite time that you admitted your need and placed your faith and trust in the redeeming work of Jesus Christ? If not, what is stopping you from making that decision? If so, how has your relationship with Christ freed you from the slavery of bitterness?

3. Complete the put off/put on chart below using one of the situations and/or people you've struggled with the most. What are the takeaways for you as you seek to overcome bitterness?

CHANGING SINFUL BITTERNESS

Put Off	Put On
Core Beliefs	Core Beliefs
1.	1.
2.	2.

Put Off	Put On
Desires	Desires
1.	1.
2.	2.
Thoughts	Thoughts
1.	1.
2.	2.
Words	Words
1.	1.
2.	2.
Behavior	Behavior
1.	1.
2.	2.

» QUESTIONS FOR GROUP DISCUSSION

1. Together, make a put off/put on chart for Esau. Share important lessons that come out of the study with other members of the group.

2. Ask someone to volunteer to tell about an area where they especially struggle with bitterness. As a group, make a put off/put on chart that expresses what is occurring on each of the five levels from both a negative and a positive perspective.

3. How does the power of the gospel impact and empower each level of the put off/put on process? What are the reasons for hope as we seek to overcome bitterness?

8

Taming a Bitter Tongue

One of the most important commodities any community should supply its residents with is a safe, reliable source of drinking water. We depend on that every day, and when it cannot be trusted, the potential negative impact on citizens cannot be overstated. We only have to look to the city of Flint, Michigan, to see an unfortunate example of that truth.[1]

In the mid-twentieth century, Flint was a growing and affluent suburb of Detroit with nearly two hundred thousand residents. It was the birthplace of many great corporations, including General Motors. Like many cities, Flint has a river flowing through the heart of town. As various industries sprouted up along the shores of the river, so did the discharge of sewage from carriage and car factories, meatpacking plants, lumber and paper mills, along with raw sewage from the city's wastewater treatment plant, agricultural and urban runoff, and toxins from leaching landfills. Some water rights activists claim that the Flint River actually caught fire—twice. When the water in your community's river is catching fire, something has gone terribly wrong.

Then, in the 1980s, rising oil prices, automobile imports, and other economic pressures resulted in the shuttering of many auto plants and their related industry. Flint's population plummeted to one hundred thousand people, with 45 percent of its remaining residents living below the poverty line. Nearly one in six homes were abandoned.

The negative impact on the city budget was staggering. In 2011, the city was placed under state control because of the pending $25 million operating deficit. The governor appointed an emergency manager to oversee and cut city costs. Most people would probably say this was a good thing, generally speaking. However, in this case a decision was made to end the city's fifty-year practice of pumping treated water from Detroit to the residents of Flint and instead begin pumping water from the Flint River. Ultimately a new pipeline was planned to carry water from Lake Huron, so the Flint River option was presented as a necessary but temporary cost-saving measure.

Almost immediately the residents began complaining that the water from their taps looked, smelled, and tasted foul. People would bring smelly, discolored jugs of water to city hall, but the officials insisted the water supply was safe. A subsequent study conducted by researchers at Virginia Tech revealed at least part of the problem—the new water source was contaminated by lead. Water samples revealed that 40 percent of the water tested measured above five parts per billion, which researchers consider an indication of a very serious problem, and 17 percent registered above fifteen parts per billion, which is the point where the federal government mandates corrective action must be taken.

Then the effects started showing up in people's health. One pediatrician reported that incidents of elevated blood lead levels in children had doubled since 2014 and had nearly tripled in certain neighborhoods. This doctor said, "Lead is one of the most damning things you can do to a child in their entire life-course trajectory."[2] The switch to water from the Flint River also coincided with an outbreak of Legionnaires' disease. Twelve people died and eighty-seven more were sickened between June 2014 and October 2015—making it the third largest outbreak in US history.

The principle is clear: exposing people to contaminated water is irresponsible and evil. If public officials do anything right, it should be to ensure a safe, fresh, clean supply of water.

It is easy to become outraged at such a betrayal of public trust. The fact that a significant percentage of Flint's residents were already in a weak and vulnerable position economically only adds to our fury.

However, the Word of God uses this exact metaphor to describe the words we allow to come out of our mouths. James pointedly says:

> But no one can tame the tongue; it is a restless evil and full of deadly poison. With it we bless our Lord and Father, and with it we curse men, who have been made in the likeness of God; from the same mouth come both blessing and cursing. My brethren, these things ought not to be this way. Does a fountain send out from the same opening both fresh and bitter water? (James 3:8–11)

Isn't it amazing that in a seminal passage on the power of our tongues, our key word bitter appears? Careful examination shows that bitterness comes up again just a few verses later in this same chapter. The principle is this: our bitter words can have the same impact on those around us as the putrid water from the Flint River had on the city's unsuspecting residents. We feel outrage at the callous irresponsibility of the public officials in Flint. Are we equally incensed at the thought that we could be doing the same thing and worse to our family, friends, coworkers, and neighbors? The good news is that the gospel is powerful enough to impact even the way we speak. The goal of this chapter is to learn how to tame a bitter tongue.

PULL OVER AND PARK

Carefully read and meditate on James 3:1–18. Be prepared to feel convicted, because these verses point out ways that we all need to change and grow. Ask the Lord to give you a spirit of humility and a deep desire to become more like Jesus. Look especially for the prominent place bitterness is given in this discussion. Does that surprise you, based on what we have learned so far in our study?

Also look for reasons to have hope. To use the parlance of Ephesians 4, these verses not only list a series of negative put-offs but an equally compelling and delightful number of put-ons. The gospel of Jesus Christ can help us speak words that are like fresh, clean water, bringing health and healing to all who hear us speak.

Recognize the Challenge of Bitter Speech

It is important for us to note how the topic of bitterness is emphasized in key places in the Word of God. Esau's bitterness and unbelief became an illustration of how the children of Israel often related to Jehovah. Bitterness is placed at the top of the list of ways to change in Ephesians 4:17–32, one of the most important passages in the entire Bible about progressive sanctification (the doctrine of Christian change and growth). Now we find the same dynamic in James 3. In what is arguably one of the most forceful and convicting texts about the power of our tongues, bitterness is repeatedly mentioned. If we want to speak words that are like fresh, clear water, we must work to rid our hearts and lives of any and all strains of bitterness.

Bitter Speech Is a Universal Problem

None of us can say we're qualified to skip this chapter because its principles don't apply to us. James makes this point repeatedly:

- "For we all stumble in many ways. If anyone does not stumble in what he says, he is a perfect man, able to bridle the whole body as well" (3:2).
- "But no one can tame the tongue; it is a restless evil and full of deadly poison" (3:8).

This has profound implications for followers of Jesus Christ. In the last thirty days, how much focus have you placed on whether your words are pleasing to God and free of sinful bitterness?

Our Words Have Incredible Impact

James was the half brother of Jesus, and while he and his siblings did not initially believe in the Lord, he eventually accepted the truth of the gospel and became a leader in the early church. Just like Jesus was the master teacher who often used word pictures to convey powerful images, James does the same when challenging us about our speech:

- "Now if we put the bits into the horses' mouths so that they will obey us, we direct their entire body as well" (3:3).
- "Look at the ships also, though they are so great and are driven by strong winds, are still directed by a very small rudder wherever the inclination of the pilot desires" (3:4).

I have watched this happen over and over in my role as a biblical counselor. When a husband speaks bitter words of complaint against his wife, it's like watching him slap her in the face. When children pour out bitter accusations against mom and dad, the entire room is like a sea of ice.

The statistics from the Flint debacle can teach us an important lesson. Fifteen parts per billion may not sound like a very high lead count, but it can actually lead to someone's death. It only takes a few bitter words spoken in an average month to kill a marriage, a family, a workplace, or a church.

Our Words Are Notoriously Inconsistent

James then makes a stunning acknowledgment about the tongue: "With it we bless our Lord and Father, and with it we curse men, who have been made in the likeness of God;

from the same mouth come both blessing and cursing. My brethren, these things ought not to be this way" (3:9–10).

Take time to consider how you tend to speak about hurts and disappointments from the past. As you retell a story, is your narrative laced with bitter words? What about the way you speak about present challenges and trials? Is bitterness present in those conversations? Then think about how you tend to discuss your future. Is listening to you like taking a drink of fresh water or bitter? Is it possible that the way you speak about your past, present, or future is sometimes good and sometimes bad? That is the overall point James is making in these particular verses. It only takes occasional bitterness to poison a situation or relationship.

Examine the Character of Bitter Speech

"But if you have bitter jealousy and selfish ambition in your heart, do not be arrogant and so lie against the truth" (James 3:14). The flow of thought in this verse is powerful even when considered in isolation. However, sound hermeneutics (principles of Bible study) makes this verse come alive because it is set in an overall context of biblical communication. Bitter speech is often part of a sinful amalgam of attributes that displease God, and James 3:14 lists four of the most significant ones.

Jealousy

Bitter jealousy—allow those words to sink deep into your heart and soul. The longer I serve as a pastor, the stronger I believe in the importance of this pairing. Why would a woman make bitter comments about a coworker? Because she is jealous of something the other person possesses. Why would a man say bitter things about his neighbor? Because that individual has a nicer yard, a bigger truck, or a fancier deck.

Thankfully, it doesn't have to be this way. You and I can choose to begin our days by thanking God for what he has given us in Christ. We can praise him for our strengths and weaknesses, as well as for the strengths and weaknesses of those around us. Jealousy is like the lead in Flint's water. The gospel is a new and pure water source that leads to thanksgiving and praise. Such fresh water will be a delight to our Lord and a source of refreshment to those around us.

Selfish Ambition

"But if you have bitter jealousy and *selfish ambition in your heart*," our verse goes on to say. The amalgam is growing. We become sinfully bitter if our goals and plans are being thwarted in some way. The dilemma is multiplied if someone close to us achieves something that we wanted faster and better than we have.

In his commentary on James 3:14, John MacArthur remarks:

> Those whose lives are based on and motivated by human, ungodly wisdom are inevitably self-centered, living in a world in which their own personal ideas, desires, and standards are the measure of everything. Whatever and whoever serves those ends is considered good and friendly; whatever and whoever threatens those ends is considered bad and an enemy. Those who are engulfed in self-serving worldly

wisdom resent anyone or anything that comes between them and their own objectives.[3]

This too is a place where the gospel can radically impact our heart at the level of our core beliefs and desires. "The good man out of the good treasure of his heart brings forth what is good; and the evil man out of the evil treasure brings forth what is evil; for his mouth speaks from that which fills his heart," Jesus explained (Luke 6:45). The cross leads us to a life of self-denial in which our selfish ambitions can be replaced with pursuing the plans and will of our Savior. "I have been crucified with Christ; and it is no longer I who live, but Christ lives in me; and the life which I now live in the flesh I live by faith in the Son of God, who loved me and gave himself up for me" (Gal. 2:20). Bitter jealousy and selfish ambition can be replaced with joyful thanksgiving and selfless motivation to love God and others.

I have the privilege of seeing this approach fleshed out by my church's leadership team on a regular basis. Faith Church has forty-two deacons, fourteen pastors, and fourteen pastoral interns who meet together monthly to pray and discuss how best to shepherd and lead the flock the Lord has entrusted to us. Over the thirty-two years I have served at Faith, I have been struck at the sweet unity the Lord has given us. That doesn't mean we never disagree, because discerning the Lord's will can be challenging this side of heaven while we're all wrestling with the curse of sin. But what impresses me is that rarely if ever are bitter words present. We can be crucified with Christ and communicate in a way that avoids both jealousy and selfish ambition. I praise the Lord for such leaders, and most of all for a Savior who makes such living possible.

Pride

James goes right for the spiritual jugular when he next says, "But if you have bitter jealousy and selfish ambition in your heart, *do not be arrogant.*" Wow. This is a hard but important truth. Bitter people often want to come off as humble, passive victims. To be sure, a person may have suffered greatly, which is why I spent so much time in earlier chapters discussing lament and the important place of bitter tears.

However, many times pride is in the background when bitter words are spoken. Frequently the bitterness begins after someone fails or disappoints us. We rehearse their shortcomings in our head, then broadcast their misdeeds with our words to anyone who will listen. Yet there's something foul in what we're saying. There's often no consideration in our heart of the fact that we fail too. We are so focused on what the other person did or didn't do that we act as if we have no failures of our own. Humble people are far less likely to speak bitter words.

The gospel comes to our rescue yet again. Consider the purpose and power of the Lord's Table that we celebrate regularly with our brothers and sisters in Christ. It is noteworthy that no bitter herbs are present as in the Jewish Passover celebration. Perhaps that's because the finished work of Jesus Christ far outshines bitter circumstances of heart and life. Regardless, we are reminded of the price that had to be paid for our sin. For our failures. For our misdeeds and shortcomings. Yes, it is a celebratory moment, but it is also a humbling one. As our pride is washed away by the reminder of the shed blood of Jesus, our temptation to speak bitter words should follow right behind.

Lies

Bitter words are filled with half-truths and complete falsehoods. That's why James completes his thought by affirming: "But if you have bitter jealousy and selfish ambition in your heart, do not be arrogant and *so lie against the truth*."

We saw that dynamic powerfully play out in the life of Esau. As he "cried out with an exceedingly great and bitter cry," he said his brother Jacob took away his blessing (Gen. 27:34–36). Wow, that was a whopper. That's what bitterness does—it makes liars out of us. Our words don't just poison those around us—they poison our own heart and soul as we repeat that narrative over and over to ourselves.

PULL OVER AND PARK

Take out a pad of paper and list specific examples of bitter words you say to yourself or others. Write them down exactly as you typically say them. Next, evaluate them in light of the four categories we see in James 3:14. Write J next to any statement that springs from jealousy, SA for speech that comes from selfish ambition, and so on. Consider how the gospel can and should empower you to use words that are the exact opposite of what is represented on your list.

Understand the Source of Bitter Speech

Surely by now most of us are highly motivated to give this area of our heart and life serious consideration. But if not, what James teaches next will undoubtedly push us across the line.

When It Is Wrong

"This wisdom is not that which comes down from above, but is earthly, natural, demonic" (James 3:15). Our adversary the devil is the father of lies and is delighted when we speak words that are false, proud, jealous, and motivated by selfish ambition. In that sense our bitter words glorify him instead of glorifying Jesus. Few things could be worse than that. No wonder James tells us that "the tongue is a fire, the very world of iniquity; the tongue is set among our members as that which defiles the entire body, and sets on fire the course of our life, and is set on fire by hell" (3:6).

This demonic source plays itself out in three different types of bitter speech. First, it can involve our evaluation of a past event. Bitterness invariably skews our circumstances, which is why, for example, the children of Israel remembered their slavery in Egypt as having pots full of meat and plenty of bread (see Exod. 16:3). The same happens when we exaggerate the evil someone did to us in days gone by. Beware of the falsehoods that are often spawned in a bitter heart.

Second, the fires of hell can produce false evaluations of our present difficulties. "The sons of Israel said to them, 'Would that we had died by the LORD's hand in the land of Egypt, when we sat by the pots of meat, when we ate bread to the full; for you have brought us out into this wilderness to kill this whole assembly with hunger'" (Exod. 16:3). That sounds like something Esau would have said. I have no doubt the Israelites were hungry. But believing they were about to die of hunger? What an offensive comment to make about their all-sufficient God.

Third, earthly wisdom leads us to irrational fears about the future. Bitter words can produce all sorts of paralyzing fears that hinder us and others from taking the steps God desires.

When It Is Right

Thankfully, there's wisdom from another source to fuel and guide the words we speak. James calls it "the wisdom from above" (3:17). Our Lord himself is a fountain of living water (John 4:10–14), and he offers to sanctify and cleanse us "by the washing of water with the word" (Eph. 5:26). This process can be so thorough that Jesus even promises that "he who believes in Me, as the Scripture said, 'From his innermost being will flow rivers of living water'" (John 7:38). Our resulting words can be free from bitterness because of the purity and sweetness of the divine source.

Be Challenged by the Effects of Bitter Speech

The old adage "sticks and stones may break my bones but names will never hurt me" is seriously flawed. Solomon had it right when he taught that "death and life are in the power of the tongue" (Prov. 18:21).

When It Is Wrong

James completes his admonition against bitter, sinful speech by explaining that the net effect of such words is "disorder and every evil thing" (James 3:16). That's exactly what the writer of Hebrews affirms when he says that a root of bitterness left unaddressed will spring up, cause trouble, and defile many (Heb. 12:15).

Bitter words will ruin a marriage. They will ruin a family. They will ruin a workplace. They will ruin a neighborhood. They will ruin a church. That's what our adversary wants to happen because he loves disorder and every evil thing.

When It Is Right

Praise the Lord for the alternative. He stands ready to help us tame our bitter tongue. The process is hard, but the fruit is more than worth it. "But the wisdom from above is first pure, then peaceable, gentle, reasonable, full of mercy and good fruits, unwavering, without hypocrisy. And the seed whose fruit is righteousness is sown in peace by those who make peace" (James 3:17–18).

Just as the devil is glorified by bitter words and their ruinous effects, our Lord is glorified when we allow him to give us the strength and direction to speak and act differently. Godly words can build a marriage. They can build a family. They can build a workplace. They can build a neighborhood. They can build a church. That is what our Savior desires because he loves righteousness that is sown in peace by those who make peace.

» QUESTIONS FOR PERSONAL REFLECTION

1. On a scale of 1 to 10, how would you rate yourself on the issue of bitter speech? Is this an area that needs work? How and in what ways?

2. Are your words sometimes characterized by jealousy, selfish ambition, pride, or lies? How are those characteristics connected to bitterness?

3. Do you struggle more with speaking bitter words about your past, your present, or your future? What steps do you need to take to address the challenges?

» QUESTIONS FOR GROUP DISCUSSION

1. Do you agree that sinful communication is a universal problem? Share examples with the group of the negative impacts you've observed from bitter words being spoken.

2. Brainstorm how and why bitterness is related to jealousy, selfish ambition, pride, or lies. What does the interplay look like?

3. How does the gospel free us to tame our tongues? What are some of the practical steps? How and where does accountability fit into the discussion?

9

God Can Help You Overcome Bitterness

One of the delightful aspects of the gospel is that God can help anyone change. A saying I frequently use with our church family is that the Lord will meet you wherever you are, but he has no intention of leaving you there. Both halves of that statement can bring incredible hope and healing as we seek to overcome bitterness of heart and life.

Think of it—the Lord will meet us wherever we are. That means if we're struggling with any aspect of bitterness that's been outlined so far in our study, we don't have to wonder if the Lord is willing and able to engage with us in our time of need. We don't have to run, hide, or attempt to blame our bitterness on someone else. Let's face it—God knows. Yet he chooses to love and move toward us anyway.

The news becomes even sweeter when we understand that our God also has a plan for our growth and sanctification. He has no intention of leaving us in our bitter condition. We can truly get to a far better place in our intimacy with God and a far sweeter place in our goal of becoming more like Jesus Christ.

It's Time to Put Our Bitterness Principles to the Test

For eight chapters now, we have studied a series of truths from Scripture about how to overcome bitterness. Multiple times I've encouraged you to "pull over and park" so you can apply these biblical ideas to the challenges you have faced in the past, are facing today, or might face tomorrow.

Often it helps to unpack a case study to see the ideas in action. That's what we will do for the remainder of the book—show how God helped a woman overcome one of the worst cases of bitterness in all of the Bible. We will do so through an applicational study of the book of Ruth—a book that provides a wonderful example of how God can help anyone overcome bitterness. I also love the story because Jesus is present in ways that are filled with hope.

Our focus in chapters 9–12 will be to demonstrate how we can find great hope and practical wisdom for moving from bitterness to faith. We'll encounter a woman whose story begins with a request that everyone call her bitter and ends with a smile on her face and a baby on her knee. And not just any baby, by the way, but a baby in the line of the Messiah. However, let's not get ahead of ourselves. First, we need to dig into Ruth 1 and uncover five ways God stands ready to help us overcome bitterness.

PULL OVER AND PARK

Take a few moments and carefully read Ruth 1. Put yourself in Naomi's shoes. Imagine what it would have felt like to experience this series of circumstances. Look for hints about Naomi's core beliefs. What is her view of trials? What is her view of her God? What is the significance that all this occurred during the time of the judges?

Picture Ruth, her young Moabite daughter-in-law. How is she different from Naomi, and why? Read Ruth 1:15 repeatedly, because it is the key verse in the chapter. Imagine what it was like when they entered the city of Bethlehem together. Listen to the exchange between Naomi and her former friends. How is Naomi like Esau? Read the last sentence in Ruth 1 several times. Can you say "cliffhanger"? Because bitterness never gets the last word.

Face the Reality of Bitter Circumstances

First of all, God will help us overcome bitterness if we will honestly acknowledge what is happening. Scripture does not sugarcoat life, and neither should we. The book of Ruth opens with a powerful illustration of the kind of bitter circumstances we discussed back in chapters 1–2. Remember that bitterness in the Bible often begins with something that happens *to* you. Just like Joseph's brothers shot bitter arrows at him, or the Egyptians placed the Israelites in bitter working conditions, or Hannah's rival provoked her bitterly— Naomi and Ruth find themselves in some of the bitterest circumstances imaginable. The Lord wants us to face that.

Lawless Days

It is important to note that these events unfolded during the days of the judges. In our English Bibles, we simply have to look back to the previous page to read the summary of that unfortunate time in the history of God's chosen nation.

The writer sadly concludes, "In those days there was no king in Israel; everyone did what was right in his own eyes" (Judg. 21:25). Interestingly, in the Hebrew Bible the book of Ruth follows the book of Proverbs, perhaps to show the relationship between the excellent wife of Proverbs 31 and the excellence of Ruth. The point to remember here is that what Naomi was as an individual, Israel was as a nation. No one had a king, not in any kind of genuine, personal sense. So they responded to trials and difficulties in ways that seemed right in their own eyes. That path always leads to bitterness.

This too has to be faced. Ask yourself, *Am I in this situation because of the lawlessness or rebellion of myself or others in my life?* If so, it's important to own up to that significant reality.

Empty Pantries

Ruth 1:1 reveals that there was a famine in the land of Judah, so Naomi's family left their village of Bethlehem and went to the land of Moab. The name Bethlehem literally means "house of bread." However, the Lord had allowed his people to face a period of trying circumstances, experiences the writer of Hebrews later describes as fatherly discipline (Heb. 12).

Most of us have probably never faced true hunger for an extended period of time. We would do well to carefully think about what this must have been like for this small Jewish family before harshly judging any of the choices they made.

Emptiness comes in many forms. For example, your pantry may be full, but your list of genuine friends may be near zero. Just like the Lord is honest about what this family was facing, you and I will only move toward the Lord if we acknowledge our need.

Playing with Fire?

Even before we learn the names of the key characters in the book of Ruth, the writer gives the shocking news that a Jewish man responds to the famine by moving his family to the country of Moab. The Bible is silent on whether this action displeased the Lord, and we dare not read more into the text than the details we are given. However, John Piper makes the important observation that "Moab is a pagan land with foreign gods (Ruth 1:15; Judges 10:6). Going to Moab was playing with fire. God had called his people to be separate from the surrounding lands."[1]

Ruth 1:2 completes the introduction by telling us the names of the family members: "The name of the man was Elimelech, and the name of his wife, Naomi; and the names of his two sons were Mahlon and Chilion, Ephrathites of Bethlehem in Judah. Now they entered the land of Moab and remained there."

How would you evaluate yourself at facing the reality of the bitter circumstances in your life? I know that I sometimes prefer to turn up the music, run faster, or look the other way. The problem with such an approach is that God's help is only available if we do what the introduction of this book leads us to—face the reality of bitter circumstances head-on.

Grinding Affliction

Naomi's bitter circumstances increase dramatically and quickly. Elimelech dies, and her two sons marry Moabite women before they also die. Ruth 1:5 makes the somber pronouncement, "And the woman was bereft of her two children and her husband."

So far, the book has been entirely silent about this family's personal relationship with the God of Israel. There's no mention of Elimelech seeking God's will before moving to Moab. That doesn't mean it did not occur, but the silence is deafening. The same is true when the sons marry Moabite women. Crickets. After the men die, it would have been an ideal time for Naomi to cry out to God in mournful lament because she recognized him as her great and gracious king. Even in her painful grief, she could have turned her eyes to heaven and poured out her heart's cries, questions, and complaints. If any of these appropriate responses to bitter circumstances did occur, the writer chooses not to record them. The more likely explanation is that in her pain, Naomi responded to grinding affliction with beliefs, desires, thoughts, words, and actions that were "right in her own eyes," because just as there was no king in Israel, there was no king in her own heart and life.

Red Stuff or Birthright?

As I said earlier, we dare not judge this family harshly without knowing all the facts. However, we have to wonder how many people in God's chosen nation during the time of the judges were living like Esau? When Elimelech moved his family, was he focusing on the red stuff of immediate satisfaction wherever it could be obtained or the birthright of trusting God even when it was hard? When Mahlon and Chilion made their marital choices, were they red-stuff decisions or birthright decisions?

Now Naomi's world is shattered with grief and hardship. It is one of those life-defining moments to declare the identity and character of one's king. But alas, "in those days, there was no king in Israel; everyone did what was right in his own eyes" (Judg. 21:25).

Wow. Isn't it refreshing and amazing to see the honesty of the Word of God? This kind of authenticity is a key step to positioning ourselves to receive God's help to overcome our bitterness. One of my favorite Scripture passages is Psalm 61:1–2: "Hear my cry, O God; give heed to my prayer. From the end of the earth I call to You when my heart is faint; lead me to the rock that is higher than I." The only way we can learn and experience what it is like for God to be our rock is to cry out to the Lord and admit that our heart is faint. We have to face it.

Understand How a Bitter Heart Is Molded

We grieve as we read what Naomi and her two daughters-in-law experienced. However, even while showing the appropriate amount of sympathy and compassion to these dear women, we still have to let the passage speak. We know that by the end of chapter 1, Naomi is instructing her former friends to just call her Bitter. Surely that response is displeasing to God. The question before us now is, what else can we learn in Ruth 1:6–19 to explain how that shockingly deep bitterness of heart and life developed?

Believing in God's Sovereignty Is Not Enough

I realize that some might argue that Naomi speaks about God in these verses. While that is partially true, there's a significant difference between speaking about God and speaking to God. There's an equally significant difference in speaking about God in a limited, skewed fashion and speaking about him in a robust, complete way.

Naomi acknowledges, at least in the way the writer records this part of the story, that "the LORD had visited His people in giving them food," and she begins traveling back to Bethlehem (1:6). She tells her daughters-in-law to return to their mothers' houses with the prayer that "the LORD deal kindly with you as you have dealt with the dead and with me" (1:8). She goes on to pray, "May the LORD grant that you may find rest, each in the house of her husband" (1:9).

Read those statements again carefully, and begin to connect the dots that lead to a bitter heart. If the daughters-in-law return to their mothers' houses in Moab and marry Moabite men, what god will they serve? The answer is shockingly obvious: Chemosh, the idolatrous god of Moab. In Naomi's heart, Jehovah had let her down, and her daughters-in-law were just as well off worshiping the god of Moab. In those days there was no king in Israel; everyone did what was right in their own eyes.

The challenging reality here is that a person can talk about God and even emphasize certain attributes of God without believing he is a good and rightful king. The cracks in our theology will be small at first—they certainly are in the case of Naomi. However, they are clearly there, and they are about to become far worse. Do you see how a bitter heart is molded?

Focusing on Your Own Resources Alone

Both daughters-in-law initially reject Naomi's suggestion. This too would have been an ideal time for the older Jewish woman to lead these two young ladies to the throne of God's exclusive goodness and grace. She could have rehearsed the covenant promises given to Israel through Abraham. Naomi could have told them about the crossing of the Red Sea or the conquest of the promised land. She could have reviewed the story of Rahab the harlot and the miraculous fall of the city of Jericho.

However, that isn't how bitter people talk. Instead, Naomi reminds them of her own lack of resources: "Have I yet sons in my womb? . . . If I should even have a husband tonight and also bear sons, would you therefore wait until they were grown? Would you therefore refrain from marrying?" (1:11–13).

This is what happens when we respond to bitter circumstances without a firm and growing faith in our rightful King. Invariably we look at our own resources and find them lacking. A bitter heart is being molded further.

Failing to Believe in God's Essential Goodness

The gloves come off at the end of Ruth 1:13, as Naomi complains, "It is harder for me than for you, for the hand of the LORD has gone forth against me." Now we can clearly see the flaws in Naomi's core beliefs about the character of God. Yes, she believes in God's sovereignty, but she does not believe in his goodness. He is not her king in any practical sense, because in her mind he is not qualified to be.

The climax of Naomi's unbelief is on full display in Ruth 1:15. Read it as many times as necessary for the point to become crystal clear. After Orpah takes Naomi up on her offer but Ruth refuses, listen to the words of this older Jewish woman: "Then she said, 'Behold, your sister-in-law has gone back to her people *and her gods*; return after your sister-in-law.'"

There it is in living Technicolor. *Any old god will do. My God let me down. He hasn't given me what I believe I need right now because fundamentally he is not good and is not worthy of my trust.*

PULL OVER AND PARK

This is a crucial point in our study to begin connecting the dots. Take out a sheet of paper and list how Naomi's words illustrate the primary principles we have learned together. In what ways is Naomi like Esau? Do you see any focus on her birthright, her place in the plan and program of the God who has revealed himself in power and glory to the Jewish people in a significant number of ways by this point in history? How is she like the "root bearing poisonous fruit and wormwood" that Moses warned about in Deuteronomy 29, that would turn the hearts of the people after other gods? How does she illustrate the principles articulated in Hebrews 12? Could she just as easily have been used as an example by the writer of Hebrews after he warns, "See to it that no one comes short of the grace of God; that no root of bitterness springing up causes trouble, and by it many be defiled" (Heb. 12:15)?

Where do you fit into this story? In your disappointment and hurt, do your desires, thoughts, words, and actions reveal a lack of belief in the goodness of God?

Rejoice in the Hope of a Sweet Alternative

I wish we could be having this part of the conversation over a cup of coffee. Your story has unique details, and so does mine. However, please keep in mind what the apostle Paul says about stories like Naomi's. God recorded them in his Word for people just like us. And what was the reason Paul gave? So that we would have hope (see Rom. 15:4).

I realize you might be thinking, *But this isn't very hopeful.* At the risk of sounding like your mom, just be patient. The story isn't over. It isn't even close to being over.

Listen to sweet Ruth. "But Ruth said, 'Do not urge me to leave you or turn back from following you; for where you go, I will go, and where you lodge, I will lodge. Your people shall be my people, and your God, my God'" (1:16). That kind of simple, quiet trust is the antidote for bitterness. It expresses trust in and commitment to not just God's sovereignty but also his fundamental goodness. She even goes on to say, "Where you die, I will die, and there I will be buried. Thus may the LORD do to me, and worse, if anything but death parts you and me" (1:17).

Did you notice the name Ruth uses for God? Is it Chemosh, the god of Moab? Not even close. She has fully embraced the salvation and new life available in the God of Israel. He is her God and is absolutely worthy of her joyful trust.

This portion of the chapter is dripping with hope. You might be at a point in life where you barely know the Lord. Perhaps you didn't grow up in a Christian home or around the things of God. Or maybe you did have a Christian upbringing, but you've ignored and rejected much if not all of it.

Listen, you can't be any greener than Ruth was. And that's the point. Ultimately this book of the Bible isn't about Naomi or Ruth. It's about the rightful King of Israel who can transform a young Moabite woman into a picture of delightful faith. He stood ready to do that for anyone living during the time of the judges, and he stands ready to do it for us and in us as well.

Avoid the Sounds of a Bitter Tongue

Remember our study of bitter speech in chapter 8? There's no better example in the Bible of what that sounds like than Naomi's words when she returns to Bethlehem. The entire passage is startling. Such words must be avoided if we are going to let the Lord help us overcome bitterness.

Unrecognizable?

When Ruth and Naomi make their entrance, "all the city was stirred because of them" (1:19). Keep in mind that this is the little town of Bethlehem. That these events unfold on the very streets where our Savior would someday be born is significant, for sure. Apparently it didn't take much to stir things up, and the women who had grown up around Naomi and her family ask a curious question: "Is this Naomi?" Why did they not recognize one of their own? We can't know for sure, but I've often wondered if it was because over time bitterness altered her appearance. Have you ever known someone who just looked bitter? That outfit is never worn well.

Full-On Bitterness

There's no room for doubt about the meaning of Naomi's answer. She says to the women of Bethlehem, "Do not call me Naomi; call me Mara, for the Almighty has dealt very bitterly with me" (1:20). In other words, "The single word in our entire language that best describes me is the word *bitter*. Mark me down as being a person whose fundamental characteristic is bitterness."

Do you say things like this? As you wrestle with bitterness, does the way you describe yourself and your situation move you closer to the Lord or farther away? "Death and life are in the power of the tongue," Solomon explained (Prov. 18:21). That includes the way we speak about what is happening around us, in us, and to us.

Remember the Issue of Deception?

At several key points, we have noted how bitterness will make liars out of us. Esau bitterly complained that his brother stole his birthright, when the truth was that he sold it. According to Ephesians 4:22, the desires of our heart can be "lusts of deceit." James tells us that "if you have bitter jealousy and selfish ambition in your heart, do not be arrogant and so lie against the truth" (James 3:14).

Did you note Naomi's two whoppers in Ruth 1:20? First, she claims that she had "gone out full." Not exactly, for it had been during a time of famine. Bitterness causes us to exaggerate about "the good ole days," just like the children of Israel spoke in glowing terms about their time of enslavement in Egypt, where they supposedly had an endless supply of food.

Even worse is the second part of Naomi's lie: "the Lord has brought me back empty." Who was faithfully standing right next to her? I have often wondered how Ruth felt when she heard those stinging words. Remember how the book of Hebrews teaches us that bitterness will cause trouble and defile many? Bitter lies like these are often the way that dynamic unfolds.

159

Bitterness Doesn't Have the Last Word

The question for each of us is clear: Are we more like Naomi or Ruth? Ask yourself, *Are there any Naomi-like tendencies in me?* If the answer is yes, take heart. God is a forgiving God who loves to hear the heartfelt confessions of a repentant person. "He who conceals his transgressions will not prosper, but he who confesses and forsakes them will find compassion" (Prov. 28:13). Also remember that the book of Ruth has four chapters, not one. Chapter 1 closes with the words, "And they came to Bethlehem at the beginning of barley harvest" (1:22). The God of hope is about to be placed on full display.

» QUESTIONS FOR PERSONAL REFLECTION

1. What's your name? If you or someone close to you were to choose one word that describes the way you live, what would it be? Is Marah/Bitter ever on the list?

2. How shocking is it to you that Naomi told her daughters-in-law to go back to their Moabite gods? In your interactions with people, do you tend to focus their hope and adoration on Jesus Christ and everything that is available in and through him, or do you point them somewhere else?

3. Do you ever tell yourself or others lies in order to justify your bitterness? Does Ruth 1:20–21 sound in any way familiar to you?

» QUESTIONS FOR GROUP DISCUSSION

1. Discuss how the events of Ruth 1 illustrate the principles we have already learned in the first eight chapters of this book. What are some of the ways you can begin connecting the dots?

2. How and why does Ruth's role in Ruth 1 give you hope?

3. Discuss the place that core beliefs, desires, thoughts, words, and actions have in the bitterness process. Find as many examples in Ruth 1 as possible.

10

The Alternative of Sweet Faith

If you've ever had the privilege of traveling to another country, you've probably also gone through some sort of customs process. Often when I travel internationally, I proceed through that part of the airport by myself because the people scheduled to meet me have to wait on the other side of customs until I have been cleared.

I'm not a particularly fearful person, but there are aspects of that experience that make me somewhat uncomfortable. Sometimes there is no heating or air conditioning, so I have been in situations where I was sure I was going to freeze solid before I got through, and other times where I was sure I was going to melt. Then there is the sheer length of the lines, where you have no idea how long it will take. Sometimes there are personnel who don't speak your language placing documents in your hand that you are supposed to complete, but they are printed in a different language or ask for information you don't have.

Some countries have a strong police or military presence, with officers carrying machines guns and leading trained dogs. We are simply not used to seeing sights like that at airports in the United States, and it can be disconcerting. However, if that is what's required to go to another country to minister the Word of God, you do what you have to do. After all, it's not like complaining will get you anywhere, because there's no alternative. Or is there?

Last summer I was scheduled to speak in a Latin American country, and as the plane landed, I was trying to prepare mentally for the hassle that was about to occur. Surprisingly, there were three well-dressed airport personnel standing just outside the plane holding a sign with my name on it. One person offered to carry my luggage while another asked if my flight had been satisfactory. They whisked me past the long lines and ushered me into a well-appointed lounge with comfortable seating and a generous spread of food. One person offered to pour my coffee while another took my passport for a cursory check. Within minutes I was approved to leave and taken to a special side door where a car was waiting to usher me to my hotel.

Apparently this treatment is intended for foreign diplomats and dignitaries, but somehow my hosts had arranged it for me. Now that I have experienced both approaches to clearing customs, I have concluded that if I ever have a choice, I prefer the VIP treatment. Up until that day, I never knew there was another option.

Ladies and Gentlemen, We Have a Card with Your Name on It!

For many people, bitterness feels like home. It is what they have known for years or even decades. They have always been jealous about certain situations. They have always been bitter with an extended family member. A low-grade seething anger has accompanied them as long as they can remember.

Perhaps you feel like there really is no alternative to bitterness in your situation. Just like the long lines and challenging circumstances at the average customs checkpoint, you just deal with it because there's no other way. Welcome to Ruth 2. The Lord Jesus Christ is standing at the doorway of the jet bridge, holding a sign with your name on it. Seriously, *your name and your name alone*. It is written in delightful calligraphy, and you better believe it's spelled correctly. The best part is the reassuring smile of the Person holding the sign. It is time to bypass the bitterness queue and take a ride on the sweet faith express. Once you embrace the alternative, you will never go back to bitterness again.

PULL OVER AND PARK

You know the drill by now. Take time to read Ruth 2. What do you make of Ruth's request to go out and glean for food? Where does she get that outrageous idea? What is she risking as a Moabite widow? How are her actions different from the prevailing approach to life in Israel, where there was no king so everyone did what was right in their own eyes? How does Jehovah respond to Ruth's choices?

What lesson do you think God was trying to teach his people? What lesson do you think God was trying to teach Ruth? What lesson do you think God was trying to teach Naomi? What lesson do you think God is trying to teach you?

Ruth 2 is all about the kind of faith in God that was absent in Naomi's life in Ruth 1. In these marvelous verses we find three characteristics of faith that overcomes bitterness.

Sweet Faith Takes God at His Word

Ruth 1 ended with the cliffhanger of Ruth and Naomi arriving in Bethlehem at the beginning of barley harvest. I hope this comes across as respectfully as I intend it: *God often has a flair for the dramatic*. Ruth 2 opens by simply stating that Naomi's husband had a close relative in town whose name was Boaz, a significant detail that will soon be explained in remarkable ways. The narrative continues in 2:2, which reports that "Ruth the Moabitess said to Naomi, 'Please let me go to the field and glean among the ears of grain after one in whose sight I may find favor.'"

In the Way Ruth Trusts the Principle of Gleaning

Gleaning was an Old Testament provision for the poor and disenfranchised. For example, in Deuteronomy 24:19 we read:

> When you reap your harvest in your field and have forgotten a sheaf in the field, you shall not go back to get it; it shall be for the alien, for the orphan, and for the widow, in order that the LORD your God may bless you in all the work of your hands.

Ruth easily could have responded to the way Naomi treated her or the difficulty of her situation by becoming even more embittered than her mother-in-law. She too could have concluded that Jehovah was unworthy of her trust. However, God empowers Ruth to take an incredible step of faith as a young widow. She places her trust in a principle from God's Word and moves in the direction of seeking his honor, glory, and blessing.

What might that look like in your particular situation? Perhaps there's a breach between you and another person, and you know God's Word commands you to go and speak to that individual. Is it time to embrace that alternative? Ask God for the faith necessary to take a step that is hard. Doing so might be exactly what you need to begin moving away from the enslavement of a bitter heart and life.

You may have been avoiding church for years because of a trial that has soured your desire to worship. Decide now that you will walk into church this coming Sunday and praise Christ because you are both invited and commanded to do so. Our Lord died on the cross and was resurrected from the grave so we could glorify him by taking him at his word. Ruth's simple step of trust is a key turning point in what the Lord does next. In the same way, your decision to return to the Lord's house could be the exact step he wants you to take. Yes, it will require faith, but Ruth's example presents a compelling alternative to living by our own thoughts and desires apart from Scripture.

Even as a Foreigner

There are strong racial overtones in this story. It's amazing to observe how often Ruth's ethnicity is mentioned. She is not just Ruth; she is clearly labeled as a foreigner.

- "Ruth the Moabitess" (2:2)
- "The young Moabite woman" (2:6)

- "Since I am a foreigner" (2:10)
- "You left your father and your mother and the land of your birth, and came to a people you did not previously know" (2:11)

It would appear that the Lord is making a powerful point for his people and for us. The person with the least exposure to God's Word and the least reason to trust his ways is the one taking the boldest step of faith. What an indictment of his own people. Yet at the same time it is a call that he stands ready to lead us to lean into his redemptive plan.

You may have concluded that bitterness is your only choice because you were not raised around people who believed in the Word of God, or because you've gotten too far off track. Ruth's story suggests otherwise. *There are no "outsiders" with God.* It wasn't just anyone who went out gleaning that day. It was Ruth the Moabitess.

Because Ruth Decides Who Is Worthy of Her Trust

What motivated Ruth to take this incredible step of faith? One of the seminal verses in the story comes when Boaz says, "May the LORD reward your work, and your wages be full from the LORD, the God of Israel, under whose wings you have come to seek refuge" (Ruth 2:12). Compare that to Naomi's suggestion in chapter 1 that Jehovah had abandoned her and that any old god would do. Ruth places her trust in the biblical principle of gleaning because she decides that Jehovah, *and Jehovah alone,* is the one whose wings are the best place of refuge.

That leads all of us to ask an important question about the fundamental nature of our relationship with God. Would those around us watch the way we live and listen to the way we talk and conclude that we are living under the shadow of God's wings? Is that where we take refuge when life is hard and people disappoint us?

PULL OVER AND PARK

Evaluate yourself in light of this marvelous phrase: "under whose wings you have come to seek refuge." Have you turned to false substitutes and placed yourself under wings where ultimate refuge will never be found? Has that inevitably led to disobedience and bitterness?

Pray to the Lord now and thank him for being a God who is ready to hear our cries of repentance and confession. Tell him you want to live under the shadow of his wings, just like Ruth. Ask him to give you sweet faith in place of bitter distrust and rebellion. Promise him that in his power you will seek to take steps to follow his Word. It probably won't mean trusting in the Old Testament principle of gleaning in your particular circumstance, but it might be something equally life-changing. What does the next step of sweet faith look like for you?

In the Way Ruth Honors Her Mother-in-Law

What is the first "manward commandment," the one that comes with a promise? "Honor your father and your mother, that your days may be prolonged in the land which the LORD your God gives you" (Exod. 20:12).

Ruth is clearly exercising faith in God's Word by honoring her Jewish mother-in-law in this way. For example, there are multiple uses of the word "cleave" in this study, including the observation in Ruth 1:14 that "Ruth clung to her." This is the same word used in Genesis 2:24 to describe a husband cleaving to his wife. Ruth's obedience to this biblical principle even becomes the talk of Bethlehem. Boaz tells her, "All that you have done for your mother-in-law after the death of your husband has been fully reported to me" (Ruth 2:11).

Next we have the delightful detail about how Ruth has a marvelous lunch and saves a portion of it for Naomi (Ruth 2:18). People whose hearts are softened by God's covenant love for them are quick to find ways to show loyal, sacrificial, compassionate love for others.

This raises the important question of how you should live if you have a person in your life who is struggling with bitterness. That may be the exact situation God has placed you in right now. Maybe your spouse or your child or an extended family member is bitter. Or maybe your boss is bitter. I don't want to minimize the pain that goes along with this challenge, because I have spoken to plenty of people in our church family and community who are called to live with this every day. However, we need look no further than Ruth 2 to see how to respond. Ruth treated Naomi with undeserved grace and compassion. That's what sweet faith does. In Paul's terminology, we overcome evil with actions that are good (Rom. 12:17–21). What might this alternative look like in your life right now?

It's true that living like this takes energy and focus. That's why it's so important to find our refuge under the shadow of God's wings. That is where we receive our strength. That is where we receive our comfort and satisfaction. And that is where we receive our direction to navigate in this fallen world. The gospel of Jesus Christ is powerful enough to make this happen. Every moment spent trusting God and following his commands is a moment that is not invested in brewing more bitterness.

In the Way Ruth Conducts Herself with Humility and Grace

We saw earlier in our study of James 3 that bitterness is often connected to pride. It makes us blind to our faults and makes us demanding of thers. Our desires and hurts take center stage, and there's no place left for God to work and his glory to be displayed. Thank the Lord for the alternative we find in the sweetness of Ruth.

- "And Ruth the Moabitess said to Naomi, 'Please let me go to the field and glean among the ears of grain after one in whose sight I may find favor'" (2:2).
- "And she said, 'Please let me glean and gather after the reapers among the sheaves'" (2:7).
- "Then she fell on her face, bowing to the ground and said to him, 'Why have I found favor in your sight that you should take notice of me, since I am a foreigner?'" (2:10).
- "Then she said, 'I have found favor in your sight, my lord, for you have comforted me and indeed have spoken kindly to your maidservant, though I am not like one of your maidservants'" (2:13).

PULL OVER AND PARK . . . WITH A TRUSTED FRIEND

This next step away from bitterness is difficult but still very important. Ask a trusted friend to help you evaluate the way you sound, especially in situations or around people with whom you're tempted to be bitter.

Slowly read the above examples of humility and grace from the lips of Ruth. Then compare your emails, text messages, and social media posts. How do your words compare to Ruth's? Do you sound humble or proud? Do you shift blame and minimize your role in the problem, or do you look for ways you may have sinned? Are your words sweet or bitter? Does anything need to be confessed to God or other people in your life? Write out better ways to speak and act when these situations arise in the future, ways modeled after what we're learning from the amazing faith of this young widow.

Sweet Faith Is Met with God's Bountiful Providence

What can we expect when we choose to move toward God in quiet trust? I hope you like barley, or whatever the equivalent blessing is in your own heart and life. Because before this chapter is over, these dear women, who had experienced terrible famine, are swimming in barley. I'm certainly not suggesting that every time you obey God's Word there will be immediate material blessings. That would be a gross perversion of the gospel. However, there is a blessedness that attends the faithful follower of Christ that is delightful to behold. Choosing the alternative of sweet faith is always worth it in the end. God wanted his Old Testament people to know that, and he wants us to know it as well.

She Just So Happened . . .

In Ruth 2:3, we read, "So she departed and went and gleaned in the field after the reapers; and she happened to come to the portion of the field belonging to Boaz, who was of the family of Elimelech." Call that a preacher joke. If you learned this story from the Kings James Version, you may remember that the translation of Ruth 2:3 states, "Her hap was to light on a part of a field belonging to Boaz." We don't talk that way now (if we ever did), but the grammar in the original language is even stronger. As one commentator explains, "The Hebrew phrase literally reads 'her hap happened,' or 'her chance chanced,' or 'she happened to happen upon.'"[1]

The point is clear: when God is the one under whose wings you come to seek refuge, you can be sure that he is working behind the scenes in ways that will astonish you. God meets Ruth's step of obedience to his Word with marvelous provision. The lesson: don't let bitterness keep you from being at the station of faithfulness when the trainload of God's bountiful provision arrives in town. Jehovah is a God of *hesed* (covenant loyalty). Why would you choose to follow any other king?

Of People Who Love God and Rejoice in His Lovingkindness

A significant part of God's provision in this story comes through a man named Boaz. Can you imagine the impact when Ruth is standing in this field and the owner walks up and addresses his workers? "Now behold, Boaz came from Bethlehem and said to the reapers, 'May the LORD be with you.' And they said to him, 'May the LORD bless you'" (Ruth 2:4).

So much for "she just happened to happen upon." God brings a man into Ruth's life who believes in Jehovah the way she does and who isn't afraid to say it right there in an open field to the people who work for him.

I understand that those who are single might feel hurt by this idea. I'm not suggesting that if you do X, Y, or Z, that God will bring a Spirit-filled spouse into your life. But if you move toward God and his people, he will bless you with the fellowship of people who love him. Part of the challenge of bitterness is that it is easy to move toward people who are equally bitter—and sometimes more so. That's a recipe for disaster. If you don't already have someone, ask God to bless you with a Christian friend who can help you nurture your trust in him.

Boaz's godliness is evidenced in part by the gracious way he speaks to Ruth. "At mealtime Boaz said to her, 'Come here, that you may eat of the bread and dip your piece of bread in the vinegar'" (2:14). She is quickly going from being a simple gleaner who has cast herself on the mercy of God to becoming an honored woman among Boaz's staff. In that culture, there was no telling what kind of abusive treatment a foreign woman might have received in this setting. God is more than able to meet our obedience and humility with abundant grace.

These Women Were "Swimming in Barley"

Who knows how long it had been since Naomi or Ruth had eaten a full meal? That's why the word "satisfied" is so delightful here.

So she sat beside the reapers; and he served her roasted grain, and she ate and was *satisfied* and had some left. . . . And [she] gave Naomi what she had left after she was *satisfied*. (Ruth 2:14, 18)

Boaz not only allows Ruth to glean but to glean among the sheaves. He even tells his workers to leave some of their own harvest on the ground for Ruth as a bonus. "So she gleaned in the field until evening. Then she beat out what she had gleaned, and it was about an ephah of barley" (2:17). At the end of that day, Ruth has gathered somewhere between thirty and fifty pounds of grain, which is comparable to a large bag of dog food in our culture. These two women could have survived for several weeks with that amount, and this was only Ruth's first day in the fields.

Pointing to an Even Greater Provision

Before this story is over, we will have a biblical laser pointing straight to our Lord and Savior Jesus Christ. The apostle John reports that Jesus said to his disciples, "I am the bread of life; he who comes to Me will not hunger, and he who believes in Me will never thirst" (John 6:35).

It is delightful to think about Ruth and Naomi enjoying this incredible provision from the hand of our merciful God. But it is far better to think about finding our own sustenance in a bountiful relationship with our loving Lord. When we move toward him in quiet trust and obedience, he will provide with sweet abundance.

Taking this back to the example of Esau, Ruth could have reached for the red stuff. She could have tried to outdo her mother-in-law's bitterness. She could have renounced her belief in God's fundamental goodness. She could have refused to consider what biblical principles might apply to her situation.

But instead Ruth reached for the birthright. She looked for refuge under the shadow of God's mighty wings. She obeyed God's Word without knowing the outcome. And she learned that while the red stuff never satisfies, the Savior always will.

Sweet Faith Acts with Courage and Trust

Are you ready for another cliffhanger? Remember that Mara—that's what Naomi had asked everyone to call her—has been watching all of this unfold. I firmly believe that by the end of Ruth 2, Naomi's bitter heart has begun to melt. Listen to her words at the end of the chapter: "Naomi said to her daughter-in-law, 'May he be blessed of the LORD who has not withdrawn his kindness to the living and to the dead'" (2:20).

Many Bible students believe that these events unfolded over a two-month period of time. What a marvelous demonstration of God's patience. Ruth's sweet faith is rubbing off on Naomi in delightful ways.

Naomi also explains to Ruth that "this man is our relative, he is one of our closest relatives" (2:20). Wait a minute. Is that a twinkle in Naomi's eye? Is she ready to trust in Jehovah's good provision again? What does she have up her sleeve? Oh, a plan is starting to take shape, one that will make even modern readers slightly blush. But that's what happens when bitterness begins to melt away. A willingness to trust and follow God with joy and boldness emerges. And you won't believe the proposal that "Mara-no-more" is about to make in Ruth 3.

» QUESTIONS FOR PERSONAL REFLECTION

1. Has bitterness hindered you from following God's Word in any specific way? What is the next logical step of obedience in your particular situation? What is stopping you from moving in that direction?

2. Reflect on times in the past when you sought to avoid sinful bitterness by following God's Word even when it was hard. What happened as a result?

3. Do you believe God will meet your attempts to obey him with abundant blessing? What might those blessings look like in your situation?

» QUESTIONS FOR GROUP DISCUSSION

1. What was Ruth risking by offering to go out and glean? What might you be risking by doing what God wants you to do today? What impact might obedience have on bitterness of heart and life? What impact might disobedience have?

2. Describe times when God has sovereignly worked at just the right time for you. How do you see God's perfect timing illustrated in Ruth 2?

3. How did God's abundant blessings impact Naomi's view of God's goodness? How does Romans 2:4 impact this discussion? Can Christians living this side of the cross ever say we are not enjoying God's abundant blessings (cf. Eph. 1:3)?

11

When Bitterness Starts Melting Away

One of my great delights as a pastor and biblical counselor is watching the Lord progressively change people into the image of Christ. As I see dramatic life changes occur in the counseling room, I'm more convinced than ever about the sufficiency of God's Word and the power of the Holy Spirit. Yes, we live in a culture that is often hardened to the gospel, but we can and should have hope because "where sin increased, grace abounded all the more" (Rom. 5:20).

There's nothing quite like watching two people who were on the verge of divorce be reconciled to God and one another. It's truly amazing when individuals who used to be at each other's throats are now holding hands and poring over Scripture together to find answers and direction for how to solve problems in their relationship. You see Christ at work when a formerly surly teenager finally opens up about his fear and disappointment, expressing a desire to communicate honestly with his mom and dad about what has been occurring.

You marvel at the Lord's grace when people struggling with depression find hope and help in the tender mercies of Jesus.

When I was preparing for pastoral ministry in Bible college and seminary, it never dawned on me that I would have so many opportunities to sit back and observe the Lord's mighty hand at work in his people. What an unexpected blessing. I firmly believe that what Paul told the Philippians is true: "For I am confident of this very thing, that He who began a good work in you will perfect it until the day of Christ Jesus" (Phil. 1:6).

We see this theme of God's power to change people on practically every page of the Bible. He is a redeeming God and is glorified by the transformational work of his Son. For example, consider the apostle Peter. I had the privilege several years ago to lead our church family through a preaching series that focused specifically on the life of Peter in the four Gospels. Week after week we marveled at the way God changed this man from a tempestuous, hardened fisherman into a godly, reliable leader in the early church. Is it any wonder that the last recorded words we have from his pen are on this very subject? "But grow in the grace and knowledge of our Lord and Savior Jesus Christ. To him be the glory, both now and to the day of eternity. Amen" (2 Pet. 3:18).

This is exactly what we see in Ruth 3. This part of Naomi's story is bubbling over with hope. Picture the end of a long, cold winter when the first warm days of spring appear. The icicles start to melt. Green vegetation begins to sprout up through the disappearing snow. The streams of cold, fresh water are roaring to life. And yes, those delightful birds are back, with their sweet songs signaling that warmer, more pleasant days are ahead. That's how patient and powerful our God is. It is time for the iceberg of Naomi's bitterness to begin melting away.

PULL OVER AND PARK

Joyfully read Ruth 3. Keep in mind that this is not just a story. This is the God of heaven and earth who orchestrated these events and then directed one of his servants to record them so people like us can hear from him. Please don't take these words lightly. You might be living with or around a bitter person right now and wondering how to navigate such a difficult relationship. Or you might be frozen in bitterness yourself and wondering if there's any hope or help for a person in your situation. Wherever you find yourself right now, this chapter of God's Word has powerful instruction for you.

As you read, put yourself in Naomi's sandals. How has her view of God changed? What is different about the way she is interpreting her circumstances? She is about to make an outrageous suggestion. Where did that come from? What is different about her heart?

Then put yourself in Ruth's position. What would you do if your Jewish mother-in-law came up with a scheme like this? Keep in mind that it is "the Lord, the God of Israel, under whose wings you have come to seek refuge" (Ruth 2:12). How does that impact your willingness to follow through with this plan?

Then turn out the lights, at least in your mind. Because what is about to happen is going to transpire in the middle of the night. Watch Boaz as he eats, drinks, and then goes to lie down at the end of the grain heap. It is time to act. What does that moment feel like? What are you saying to God as you move across the threshing floor?

Close your eyes and imagine this midnight conversation between you and Boaz. What an incredible picture of a godly man. Imagine the peace and joy that sweeps over your heart as you hear him speak. And always keep in mind, this is not just Boaz talking. This is the God of Israel who is teaching you a lesson. How does our gracious God relate to those who come to him in quiet, passionate trust?

Then prepare yourself for another cliffhanger. What happens in your heart when you hear the words, "However, there is a relative closer than I"? What can we learn about ice-melting faith at that moment?

One last sandal switch. What was Naomi doing during this time? Do you hear or see any traces of bitterness? Is her faith rewarded? I hope you like barley, because these formerly starving widows are about to receive yet another heap of it. But more than that, they are learning what happens when people believe that God is good. Really good. And fully deserving of our compassionate trust.

The Main Point

The lesson of Ruth 3: *the ice of bitterness is melted by faith that embraces and affirms God's essential goodness and acts courageously even when times are hard.* That means that if your relationship with the Lord has been frozen in bitterness and unbelief for decades, you don't have to stay that way. God stands ready with a giant container of ice melt and will sprinkle it liberally over your heart and life.

If he enabled Naomi to change from "call me Mara" in Ruth 1 to "let's trust God enough to make a wedding proposal" in Ruth 3, he can help us be dramatically different in the way we relate to him and those around us. This is what happens when you *have* a king in Israel and you do what is right in *his* eyes. In this chapter, we find three characteristics of bitterness-melting courageous faith.

Courageous Faith Is Willing to Risk

Ruth 3:1 explains what Naomi has been thinking about as she has watched God work over the past two months. She tells Ruth, "My daughter, shall I not seek security for you, that it may be well with you?" Her view of the Lord has dramatically changed. Now it is time to offer a proposal that only a woman of growing faith would consider.

By Looking for His Gracious Hand

Naomi reminds Ruth that Boaz is their kinsman (3:2). Now she is finally thinking more biblically about their situation. She knows the Lord is the one who directed Ruth to Boaz's field and is the source of the bounty they have enjoyed. This is not simply an interplay between Ruth and Boaz. It is a providential and sovereign experience between Naomi and the God from whom she has been estranged for so long.

Then Naomi hatches the plan she has probably been contemplating for weeks. Their gracious God is worthy of their trust and even of their risk. That's an important point in this narrative and for every person seeking to work out of sinful bitterness. At some point we have to take God at his word, even when we cannot see the outcome. Bitterness makes us doubt and protect; sweet faith makes us trust and risk. Ask God for the courage to follow him even when it's hard.

Naomi has thought through all the details. What Ruth should wear. Where Ruth should go. When Ruth should advance. I wish we had a video of this moment. What happened to "just call me Mara"? This woman deserves a place in the faith hall of fame. Imagine the excitement in her voice and the trust in her heart. Then pan the camera over to Ruth's face. This is one of those "I can't wait to get to heaven and ask her about this" events in the Bible. Won't it be fun to attend the "Ruth is going to tell all of us what it was like to hear Naomi's proposition" lecture?

Why is Naomi willing to make such a proposal? Because by now she has witnessed God's bountiful care firsthand. She knows God loves and cares for her and Ruth. She believes he loves her deeply and can be trusted. She is amazed that even in her darkest periods of bitterness, the Lord of Israel was watching over her. The Lord was giving her courageous faith. She now acts in a way that would later be described in the Psalms: "Be strong and let your heart take courage, all you who hope in the LORD" (Ps. 31:24).

The Power of an Example

It is important to note the relationship between what Naomi does in chapter 3 and what Ruth had already done in chapter 2 when she requested permission to go and glean. Naomi is simply following in Ruth's courageous footsteps. Ruth had trusted in a principle from God's Word, and now it's Naomi's turn. There's an essential sense in which she is placing herself under God's wings to find refuge (Ruth 2:2).

My wife and I have three children, two of whom are adopted. Our adopted son Andrew is a young adult with special needs, including blindness, autism, and a host of other mental and physical challenges. He will live with us as long as we are able to care for him, and he is a delightful member of our family in many ways. He loves bears and even likes to be called "the Bear."

Each day the Bear has a program of educational and physical exercises he performs at home, including one where he crawls around our great room on his hands and knees to work on balance and dexterity. Of course he has renamed it "the bear crawl" and has added friendly growls to the routine. The other day my wife sent me a video that showed the Bear and our two-year-old grandson, Jude, who had come over for a visit. The video showed how Jude was carefully mimicking every move the Bear made, crawling right behind him and growling and giggling all along the way. He said he wanted to be just like his Uncle Bear.

That's what happens in the book of Ruth. This young Moabite woman trusts the provision of God's Word and courageously goes out to a field and begins to glean. But she doesn't go alone. Just like Jude watches the Bear, Naomi has been watching Ruth's every move. God in his compassion and mercy meets Ruth's obedience with abundant blessing because he is fundamentally good. Naomi is motivated to take her courageous steps in chapter 3 because young Ruth blazed the trail.

A Challenge to Those Living with or around Someone Who Is Bitter

You may be reading this book primarily because the challenge God has given you during this season in life is the presence of a person who is frozen in bitterness. You may be married to that person. It may be your parent or your child.

Perhaps you have a coworker or neighbor who can hardly speak a sentence without bitterness spewing out.

That can be exhausting. Imagine what the trip from Moab to Bethlehem was like for Ruth. In chapter 1 we have just a small sample of Naomi's words. Multiply that many times over as you retrace the women's dusty steps.

Do you know the only thing worse than one very bitter person? Two very bitter people. That means that God may have placed you in this position to model courage and faithfulness. Choose to take God at his word in whatever he is calling you to do in your particular situation. To use Bear's terminology, just start bear crawling. You might have to take a few laps of obedience by yourself, but don't be surprised if you eventually look behind you and the bitter person in your life is starting to follow your example. Do you know the only thing better than one courageous person? Two courageous people, one following the other's faithful example. This may be exactly why the Lord has placed this particular bitter person in your life.

A Challenge to the Person Frozen in Bitterness

Throughout this writing project, I've prayed regularly for those who will read this book because they truly are looking for a way out of a sinfully bitter heart and life. If that is your present situation, you're an answer to prayer.

But the question now becomes, how does the Lord want Ruth 3 to impact you? It is likely that you have a Ruth-like individual in your life. If not, I would encourage you to find a good church and seek a counselor, friend, or mentor who can model sweet faith for you. Watch them do their bear crawl. Mimic their steps. Then follow their example. What truth from the Word of God do you need to act on? What principle do you need to embrace? It may not be something as outrageous as Naomi's suggestion in Ruth 3. But without a doubt, courageous faith melts icy bitterness each and every time.

I recently heard the story of a woman who has been struggling with disappointment for years. Her life just hasn't turned out the way she hoped, planned, and dreamed. She struggles with bitterness, but she is determined to not let it have the final word. She has found that several of her coworkers are also facing great difficulties, but they do not yet know the Lord. Therefore she is taking God at his word and is being an ambassador for Christ (2 Cor. 5:20), and consequently one of her coworkers asked her to go out for lunch to learn more about what it means to be a Christian. That's exactly what Ruth would have done in chapter 2 and what Naomi would have done in chapter 3. The effect that kind of courageous faith has on bitterness is marvelous and astounding.

Courageous Faith Is Rewarded by God's Good Hand

If you wonder what might happen if you choose to follow the Lord's Word even when times are hard, you don't have to look any further than the middle of Ruth 3. This is not to suggest that God blesses every person in exactly the same way at exactly the same time. But there's no way around the delightful truth that Naomi's suggestion is met with his abundant provision.

Naomi's Daughter-in-Law Is an Amazing Woman

Ruth could have said no to Naomi. In fact, I suppose she could have said no with a few expletives attached before and after. That's part of the risk Naomi was willing to take. Please don't miss that essential point. Just like Ruth took a risk in chapter 2, Naomi is taking one in chapter 3.

Also keep in mind what Naomi had said back at the end of chapter 1: "I went out full, but the LORD has brought me back empty" (1:21). What an incredible offense to sweet Ruth who was faithfully standing by her side. But now when Naomi explains her plan, Ruth's humble response is, "All that you say, I will do" (3:5).

The plan could not have gone any better. Boaz, as a wonderful example of our future kinsman redeemer the Lord Jesus Christ, treats Ruth with compassion, gentleness, and kindness.

> Then he said, "May you be blessed of the LORD, my daughter. You have shown your last kindness to be better than the first by not going after young men, whether poor or rich. Now, my daughter, do not fear. I will do for you whatever you ask, for all my people in the city know that you are a woman of excellence." (Ruth 3:10–11)

God Is Giving Naomi Time and Reasons to Change Her Mind

This entire exchange will soon be reported to Naomi. As I said earlier, imagine the God of heaven standing there with a large container of ice melt. Think back to Naomi's core beliefs about God from Ruth 1:

- "The hand of the LORD has gone forth against me" (1:13).
- "Your sister-in-law has gone back to her people and her gods; return after your sister-in-law" (1:15).

186

- "Call me Mara, for the Almighty has dealt very bitterly with me" (1:20).
- "I went out full, but the LORD has brought me back empty" (1:21).
- "Why do you call me Naomi, since the LORD has witnessed against me?" (1:21).
- "The Almighty has afflicted me" (1:21).

Now factor in all that Naomi is experiencing in Ruth 3. She takes a courageous risk and encourages Ruth to do the same. Each of the statements listed above is proving to be false. What incredible evidence of God's patience with his people.

This brings us to one of the core truths about bitterness. Naomi became bitter *because she believed God was against her*. In her own words, he afflicted her, brought her back empty, had gone forth against her, and dealt bitterly with her. Amazingly, she even told Ruth to go back and follow the Moabite god Chemosh, because in her mind, the God of Israel was unworthy of her trust. But now her core theology has changed. One tremendous effect is a willingness to trust God courageously.

PULL OVER AND PARK

Review the list of situations and people over which you find yourself struggling with bitterness. Then carefully read Romans 8:26–39. Do you really believe that "if God is for us, who is against us" (Rom. 8:31)? Do you believe that if you are a Christian, nothing can separate you from the love of Christ (8:35)? Do you believe that you can "overwhelmingly conquer through Him who loved us" (8:37)?

Is it possible that you have not taken courageous steps of faith regarding some principle of God's Word because fundamentally you have questioned God's goodness? Does your heart sound more like Naomi in Ruth 1 or Paul in Romans 8?

Write out the key verses and ideas from Romans 8:26–39. Begin committing them to memory. Look for specific situations where you can apply these truths to real-life situations. Ask the Lord for opportunities to take a step of courageous faith in his Word to prove that you are growing in your belief in his fundamental goodness.

Not Another Cliffhanger!

Boaz's integrity is on full display when he tells Ruth:

> Now it is true I am a close relative; however, there is a relative closer than I. Remain this night, and when morning comes, if he will redeem you, good; let him redeem you. But if he does not wish to redeem you, then I will redeem you, as the LORD lives. Lie down until morning. (Ruth 3:12–13)

Ahhhh! Why does Boaz have to be such an honest man? Because he loves and serves a God of truth and righteousness. He is the antithesis of the people described at the end of the book of Judges who simply did whatever was right in their own eyes. And he is also exactly what Naomi needs at the moment. She trusted God. Ruth trusted God. And now Boaz is going to trust God. What is especially delightful about all this is—bitterness is nowhere to be found.

Courageous Faith Knows When to Act . . . and When to Wait

Sometimes the greatest antidote to bitterness is to patiently wait on the Lord. While your emotions may be screaming all sorts of ideas and plans that could lead you right back into bitterness, a biblically trained heart can help you courageously act on whatever principle from God's Word is applicable at the time and then quietly wait to see what the Lord will do.

I often find myself in that position as a pastor. A significant aspect of my shepherding responsibility is talking to people about ways they need to change. Situations requiring that kind of congregational care can be stressful, and if I'm not careful, I can find myself becoming bitter because I have to "handle another problem." I have learned that if I ignore problems or let them go, in direct disobedience to what God's Word calls me to do, the bitterness gets worse. However, the man who mentored me in ministry taught me to address problems right away out of my love for God and his people. Often that puts me right in the middle of what Ruth had to do in Ruth 2 and what Naomi had to do in Ruth 3: *take a step of faith.* Schedule the meeting. Confront the problem. Speak the truth in love.

Episodes like this always draw me closer to Christ. I cry out to him for strength and help. I examine my own heart and life and try to take the log out of my eye first before trying to help someone else take the speck out of theirs (Matt. 7:1–5). I remind myself of verses like Joshua 1:9, "Be strong and courageous! Do not tremble or be dismayed, for the LORD your God is with you wherever you go." This kind of courageous obedience drives out the bitterness because the two simply cannot occupy the same space.

However, once the meeting is over and the confrontation is complete, it's time to wait. I cannot expect a person or family to always repent and ask forgiveness immediately. That's simply not the way the process usually works. So what does sweet courageous faith do in the meantime? It waits. "Wait for the LORD; be strong and let your heart take courage; yes, wait for the LORD" (Ps. 27:14).

The Provision Continues

How does the Lord treat us while we faithfully wait on him? In Ruth and Naomi's case, God blessed them with yet another load of barley. And don't you love the way Boaz phrased his instructions in 3:17? "Do not go to your mother-in-law empty-handed." Isn't that just like our Lord? The same woman who accused God of being against her. Of being no better than Chemosh. Of dealing bitterly with her and bringing her back empty. Still God rewards her steps of faith with more provision.

A Sleepless Night?

The Bible is completely silent about what Naomi did that night. After we attend Ruth's lecture in heaven about her response to Naomi's initial suggestion, then I hope Naomi is scheduled to speak. Wouldn't you love to know what she did that night? Do you think she paced the floor? Do you think she prayed to God for Ruth's protection? Do you think she slept like a baby? We'll never know this side of eternity. But in a method that is becoming all too familiar, we can almost predict what will happen next. Another cliffhanger. "Then she said, 'Wait, my daughter, until you know how the matter turns out; for the man will not rest until he has settled it today'" (3:18).

» QUESTIONS FOR PERSONAL REFLECTION

1. What would a step of courageous faith look like in your situation? Is there anything in God's Word that you know you should do but have been resisting?

2. Do you struggle with believing in God's essential goodness? Do you ever sound like Naomi in Ruth 1? How and in what ways? What needs to change?

3. Do you have people in your life who model sweet and courageous faith? Pause and thank God for them. Consider sending them a note of appreciation for the way God is using them in your life.

» QUESTIONS FOR GROUP DISCUSSION

1. Read 1 Peter 2:21–25 together. How did Jesus avoid bitterness by faithfully trusting in his Father?

2. How do various aspects of the gospel message empower us to take steps of obedience to God's Word even when life is hard?

3. Discuss and thank God for people you know who have avoided sinful bitterness by exercising risky faith. How and in what ways has God rewarded them? What are the takeaways for you?

12

Embracing God's Sweetness

In our town we have a fabulous locally owned steak restaurant called Mountain Jacks. It is known for its signature prime rib, and when a group of people want to enjoy an unusually great meal or celebrate a special occasion, Mountain Jacks is often their destination. I love this place for all sorts of reasons, including the way the meal is designed to build to a crescendo, course by delicious course.

They start by bringing a special circular salad tray to the table so the waiter can make an individually designed salad for each guest. Next, someone comes with warm bread, homemade cinnamon butter, and a marvelous soup. I always try to pace myself at that point because I don't want to fill up too quickly, but I'm a pushover for bread that has just come out of the oven. Then they deliver the main course—a generous slab of perfectly cooked prime rib along with whatever sides each guest requested. In my case, that requires additional slices of bread because, well . . . just because.

By this point, I'm feeling totally stuffed. Sometimes I even mutter, "I couldn't eat another thing." So untrue. Because the final step is when the waiter brings the dessert tray. I have heard it described so many times I could close my eyes and recite it from memory. Carrot cake with smooth buttercream icing. Cheesecake with strawberries cascading over the sides. Chocolate cake with thick chocolate icing covered with chocolate shavings.

However, very few people order any of those selections. Because I haven't told you about the best option yet. Brace yourself. It is called Mile High Mud Pie. Seriously. I love those words. It's one of those desserts that contains all the essential food groups. At least that's what I tell myself while ordering it. The base is a crushed Oreo cookie crust. Who could go wrong with that foundation? Then there's a thick layer of coffee-flavored ice cream covered by a coating of gooey fudge sauce. Next there's a generous layer of homemade whipped cream topped off with a drizzle of more hot fudge sauce and shaved almonds. As much as I enjoy the salad and the bread and the signature prime rib, I love how this restaurant always saves the very best for last.

This is essentially what happens in Ruth 4. Admittedly, the book has been marvelous thus far. If you find yourself relating to Ruth's story because you're living with a bitter person, I hope you've been encouraged by Ruth's sweet, surprising, and abiding faith. Our God can produce amazing fruit in the lives of those who follow him. If Naomi is the one whose life most closely mirrors yours, I hope you, too, are being challenged and refreshed by the way the Lord is transforming Just-Call-Me-Mara into a woman who courageously follows his will and finds her bitterness melting away.

However, this story is far from over. The waiter is here. He is describing the dessert tray. Can I recommend that you go with . . . the Mile High Mud Pie? I can't imagine a chapter in the Bible that could be packed with more sweet ingredients than Ruth 4. The lesson is clear—who would ever linger in the throes of bitterness when this kind of outcome is possible? God always saves the best for last.

PULL OVER AND PARK

Okay, it's time to reach for your fork. Be sure your napkin is positioned well because this course can get a bit sloppy. Sit back and take a deep breath. I realize the first three chapters of Ruth provided a lot of nourishment. However, trust me when I speak from vast experience on this one. You have room for dessert. Especially when it tastes this good.

Read Ruth 4. Savor each layer. Be amazed at this man Boaz. His integrity is a stark contrast to the condition of many people in Israel at that time. Close your eyes and imagine this scene. Then picture this other closer relative. I don't like him, do you? Listen to him utter those fateful words in Ruth 4:4: "I will redeem it." I think I'm going to be sick.

But keep reading. These cliffhangers never end, do they? Boaz answers him wisely, and the man offers his sandal. That has to be the sweetest sandal that has ever been removed from a person's foot.

Then listen carefully to Boaz's speech to the elders. This is not some shallow love story on cable TV. Be amazed at the explanation he gives for why he wants to be the kinsman redeemer. This is covenant language or, hearkening back to our discussion of Esau, "birthright language." Then the people in the court and the elders make a fascinating series of pronouncements. What do Rachel, Leah, Perez, Tamar, and Judah have to do with all of this?

Put your fork down for a moment and ask yourself a question: How many children did Ruth and her deceased husband, Mahlon, have during their ten-year marriage? They didn't have any. Hmmm. Read Ruth 4:13 carefully and repeatedly. Imagine her surprise. Imagine her joy. What a mighty God we serve.

Now sit back and get ready. Who becomes the focal point beginning in verse 14? Surely it would be Ruth, right? Wait a minute. Why are the women talking to Naomi in verse 14? Why is Naomi taking the child in her lap? And what do the neighborhood women say in verse 17? A son has been born to *whom*?

As if the story couldn't get any sweeter, there are a few delicious bites left. Who is this little baby? Could it be that he is the "redeemer" (v. 14)? Is he Naomi's "restorer of life" and sustainer of her old age (v. 15)? What is God trying to tell us about people who choose to move away from sinful bitterness?

Now read the final genealogy. You just rolled your eyes, didn't you? Trust me, this one is especially important. You've heard some of these names before. In fact, you probably hear them read every Christmas. Because God always saves the best for last.

As you can see, Ruth 4 is truly an amazing chapter in God's Word. In these remaining pages, let's organize the flow of thought to find three principles to fully embrace the sweetness that comes from overcoming bitterness.

God Honors People Who Do What Is Right in His Eyes

Boaz is a clear and delightful contrast to many of the people living during the time of the judges. That should give us both direction and encouragement. Part of avoiding bitterness is choosing to carefully follow the Lord's will all along the way. Ruth 4 makes it clear that our God is able to help us do just that.

He Didn't Cut Any Corners

Naomi was right in her prediction at the end of Ruth 3: "the man will not rest until he has settled it today" (3:18). Boaz goes to the city gate, where important business is transacted. When the closer relative passes by, Boaz asks him to sit while they assemble the appropriate witnesses. He carefully explains the situation and offers the man the opportunity to act on his legal rights as kinsman redeemer. Boaz doesn't try to game the system or twist the facts. He is a man of integrity.

Not Another Cliffhanger?

Next we hear the fateful words at the end of verse 4, when the closer relative announces, "I will redeem it." That's almost like finding a hair in your Mile High Mud Pie, although I can assure you that has never happened at Mountain Jacks. Thankfully, the disappointment only lasts for a moment. As Boaz explains that the closer relative would also have covenant responsibilities to "Ruth the Moabitess" (4:5), the unnamed man says, "I cannot redeem it for myself, because I would jeopardize my own inheritance. Redeem it for yourself; you may have my right of redemption, for I cannot redeem it" (4:6).

An Esau-Like Missed Opportunity?

This is a curious response indeed. The purpose of Levirate marriage in the Old Testament was to honor the deceased relative and protect his widow and children. The Mosaic law was very clear about what should be done to a man who would not fulfill his covenant responsibility:

> But if the man does not desire to take his brother's wife, then his brother's wife shall go up to the gate to the elders and say, "My husband's brother refuses to establish a name for his brother in Israel; he is not willing to perform the duty of a husband's brother to me." Then the elders of his city shall summon him and speak to him. And if he persists and says, "I do not desire to take her," then his brother's wife shall come to him in the sight of the elders, and pull his sandal off his foot and spit in his face; and she shall declare, "Thus it is done to the man who does not build up his brother's house." In Israel his name shall be called, "The house of him whose sandal is removed." (Deut. 25:7–10)

Exactly how this law might have applied at this time and in this situation is unclear, but the man's decision was definitely focused on his own desires instead of Ruth's or God's. This is yet another example of every person doing what was right in their own eyes.

This man's choice also places him squarely in line with Esau all the way back in Genesis 25. When faced with the opportunity to value his birthright, his place in God's covenant plan for his chosen people, he ignores that privilege and responsibility because of the immediate gratification that comes with another helping of red stuff.

PULL OVER AND PARK

Are you more like Boaz or the unnamed relative? Wherever you are in your current struggle with bitterness, the Lord will give you plenty of opportunities to wear Boaz's sandals. It is a choice between embracing your birthright in Christ or reaching for another batch of shortcut red stuff.

For example, you or your family may desire to purchase a larger house. Your reasons are sound because your family is growing and additional space would serve everyone well. However, you can embrace your birthright as a follower of Christ and proceed with integrity through the process or sinfully cut corners in order to achieve the prize at any cost. A Boaz-like person will carefully save, fairly negotiate, and patiently respond when the inevitable hiccups occur during the inspection and mortgage procedures. A person like our unnamed relative will rush the decision before being prepared financially, or manipulate the negotiation process, or explode in sinful anger when things don't go their way.

Another possible example is a person seeking a spouse. A Boaz-like person establishes biblical standards for dating and marriage, bathes the process in prayer, seeks wise counsel, and patiently waits for God's provision. Far too many single people act like Naomi's unnamed relative, selfishly focusing only on what they want and making shortcut red-stuff choices that result in a world of heartache and pain.

What does Boaz-like integrity look like in your current season of life? What are the short-term costs and challenges of this kind of obedience and godliness? Do you believe the Lord is powerful enough to help you live like Boaz? Do you believe God is good enough that you can and should trust his ways more than your own? Is the sweetness that comes from following him worth the wait? How will obedience keep you from bitterness? How will selfishness and impulsiveness make a bitter result more likely?

How does Jesus fit into this aspect of the story? Pause and reflect on the beauty of his statement in John 8:29—"And He who sent Me is with Me; He has not left Me alone, for I always do the things that are pleasing to Him." Can you taste the sweetness there? That sounds a lot like Boaz. Ask the Lord to help that sound a lot like you too.

Seek the Long-Range Joy of Obedience

Reaching for the birthright is always better than the immediate gratification of grabbing the red stuff. Throughout this study, we have seen the bitter fruits of Esau's rejection of his place in God's plan and purpose for his people. This profane man despised God's promises given through Abraham. His question in Genesis 25:32, "What use then is the birthright to me?" exposed his heart and defined his existence.

Boaz, in contrast, was careful, deliberate, and honorable. As Naomi moves out of bitterness, and as she and Ruth trust the God of Israel, their sweet faith is wed—in this case literally and figuratively—to the obedience and integrity of Boaz.

He Pays the Price of Redemption

"Then Boaz said to the elders and all the people, 'You are witnesses today that I have bought from the hand of Naomi all that belonged to Elimelech and all that belonged to Chilion and Mahlon'" (Ruth 4:9). Scripture is silent on whether Ruth and Naomi are actually present when this proclamation is made. Regardless, they either heard his words then or learned about them shortly thereafter.

Imagine the joy and relief that came to their hearts. God is worthy of their trust and allegiance. He is not only sovereign, he is good. Boaz, a man of integrity, pays the price for them. The path of obedience has taken them to a sweet place that Naomi's bitterness never could.

It is a very short walk for followers of Jesus Christ from the words of Boaz to the gospel of our Lord and Savior: "Knowing that you were not redeemed with perishable things like silver or gold from your futile way of life inherited from your forefathers, but with precious blood, as of a lamb unblemished and spotless, the blood of Christ" (1 Pet. 1:18–19). There's nothing sweeter to a Christian than thinking about the marvelous, sacrificial, loving price that was paid to set us free. Short-term red-stuff choices take us away from that delight—long-term birthright choices take us closer.

His Motivation Is Pure

One of the many blessings of this chapter is that we are not left to wonder why Boaz made this choice. "Moreover, I have acquired Ruth the Moabitess, the widow of Mahlon, to be my wife in order to raise up the name of the deceased on his inheritance, so that the name of the deceased will not be cut off from his brothers or from the court of his birth place; you are witnesses today" (Ruth 4:10). This is what birthright speech sounds like—concern is for the honor of God and his people. Boaz wants to carefully follow God's Word in all his dealings.

There's something amazingly sweet in listening to this man. Imagine now that Ruth and Naomi are going to have

Overcoming Bitterness

the pleasure of living with a person with this kind of love and integrity. They couldn't be more blessed. Or could they?

His Actions Are Admired and Blessed

Now those who have witnessed these events speak.

> All the people who were in the court, and the elders, said, "We are witnesses. May the LORD make the woman who is coming into your home like Rachel and Leah, both of whom built the house of Israel; and may you achieve wealth in Ephrathah and become famous in Bethlehem. Moreover, may your house be like the house of Perez whom Tamar bore to Judah, through the offspring which the LORD will give you by this young woman." (Ruth 4:11–12)

Modern readers less familiar with Old Testament history might scratch their heads at such illustrations, but these people know exactly what they are saying. Keep in mind that Ruth and her deceased husband, Mahlon, had not conceived children throughout their ten-year marriage. However, one of the stated purposes of Levirate marriage was to perpetuate the name of the deceased in some way, which means the intent is that Boaz and Ruth will have children.

Therefore the witnesses ask the Lord to bless this union with a child, just like Rachel and Leah who "built the house of Israel" (v. 11). Commentators Brad Brandt and Eric Kress suggest that the significance may be that these two women were also "non-Abrahamites—non-Jews— who left their homes pledging allegiance to Israel and his God (cf. Gen. 31:16)."[1] The witnesses then pray for Boaz, using words that literally could be translated "may you do valiantly in Ephrathah, and proclaim the name in

Bethlehem."[2] Lastly, they call everyone's attention to Israel's most famous Levirate birth—that of Perez to Judah and Tamar (see Gen. 38).

This is a bold request, but it is rooted from beginning to end in the covenant loyalty of Israel's God. Verse 11 begins with "May the LORD" and verse 12 ends with "the LORD will give you."

I realize this part of the story could call up painful memories for some readers. I'm thinking especially about someone who may have lost a child or who has been unable to conceive. There is certainly no promise here that if you seek to avoid sinful bitterness, God will give you everything you desire in this life. He blesses each of his children at different times and in different ways. Knowing that he can provide is what motivates us to continue loving and serving him, trusting that the nature and timing are best left in his good hands. The sweetness will come. God calls us to leave the details of the provision to him.

Never Give Up on Naomi, Because Our Faithful God Never Does

Just when you think this beautiful love story of redemption couldn't get any better, our Lord provides a topping of whipped cream and fudge sauce that's almost hard to believe. When the book of Ruth opened, Naomi's life was filled with emptiness, unbelief, and profound bitterness. She even told her daughters-in-law to go back to their people and their gods because the God of Israel was unworthy of their trust. But those days are long gone, and these final verses couldn't be more delicious.

The Barren Comes to Life

With an economy of words, the writer reports, "So Boaz took Ruth, and she became his wife, and he went in to her. And the LORD enabled her to conceive, and she gave birth to a son" (Ruth 4:13). We're left with dozens of questions, but the story allows no time for that. The witnesses in verses 11–12 had asked the Lord to do something, and he answers in a powerful and spectacular fashion.

The Women Said to Whom?

Now prepare yourself for a shock. This is almost like finding an extra chocolate mint inside the final scoops of whipped cream. We would have expected the women to speak to Ruth or perhaps to Boaz. But instead they focus their attention on Naomi. These may well be some of the same women who met Naomi and Ruth when they first returned to Bethlehem back in chapter 1. "Is this Naomi?" they had asked (1:19). She looked so different from when she and her family had left town. Naomi had even asked them to call her Mara, because that was the only word in her mind that defined her existence (1:20).

My, how things have changed. Now Naomi is rested, full, and bouncing a little baby on her lap. Taste the sweetness in this scene. Is God worthy of her trust? Is he not only sovereign but also good? Does he give good gifts to his people in his time and in his way? Yes, yes, and yes.

Who Is the Redeemer?

The women focus their speech on how Naomi has not been left without a redeemer. In their words, it is the Lord who should be blessed for his faithful provision. However, Bible students are somewhat divided on whether the women are speaking about Boaz or about this little baby boy. I personally believe the grammar of verses 14–15 points to the baby himself. In light of what we are about to read, his birth is far from typical. When God gives gifts, he often gives ones that are astoundingly precious.

Naomi, Naomi, Naomi

You would expect the camera to pan back to Ruth or Boaz at this point, but that isn't what happens. Verse 16 reports that "Naomi took the child and laid him in her lap." Picture her joyfully playing with him on her knee and singing him to sleep like practically every grandmother before and after.

Then an additional shock comes. "The neighbor women gave him a name, saying, 'A son has been born *to Naomi!*'" (v. 17). Say what? This is unbelievable. The focus clearly is on how God has chosen to bless this woman who has moved away from bitterness to quiet trust. What an incredible sweetness! They name the little boy Obed, meaning "servant," perhaps because as he grows up, he will serve and love his grandmother as an instrument of God's love for her.

And What a Baby He Was!

If the story stopped right here, it would be utterly amazing. God's good hand of blessing could not be any sweeter. But there's still one more bite of dessert left on your plate. It is the genealogy. This baby boy would grow up and someday have a son named Jesse. And Jesse would have a son named David—as in King David. And David would have a descendant named Jesus—as in our Lord and Savior Jesus Christ.

It is true. "Abraham was the father of Isaac. . . . Salmon was the father of Boaz by Rahab, Boaz was the father of Obed by Ruth, and Obed the father of Jesse. Jesse was the father of David the king. . . . Jacob was the father of Joseph the husband of Mary, by whom Jesus was born, who is called the Messiah" (Matt. 1:2, 5, 16).

A Word to the Ruths

Living with or around a Naomi can be an incredible challenge. Bitter people are draining as they doubt and complain and speak words that are like the putrid bile of the gall bladder. However, God stands ready to give you Ruth-like faith. Always remember that the only thing worse than one bitter person . . . is two bitter people. Keep cultivating and modeling Christlike faith. The gospel can empower and motivate you to do that even when it's hard. If you are young in the Lord yourself, take heart. So was Ruth.

Whatever you do, don't give up on the Naomi in your life. That person may seem as cold as an iceberg. They may even ask you to change their name to bitter because that is the word that best defines their existence. But God doesn't want bitterness to ever have the last word. The good news is that bitter people like Naomi can change for the glory of God in a way that directs everyone's attention to the power of God's perfect Son. We can "taste and see that the LORD is good; how blessed is the man who takes refuge in Him!" (Ps. 34:8).

A Word to the Naomis

Throughout this project, I have thought about and prayed for those who would pick up this book because their story is very similar to Naomi's. If that is true of you, I thank and commend you for reading all the way through. I hope you've been encouraged and helped by these principles. More importantly, I hope you've grown more in your love for God. He is good and is worthy of your trust.

One final thought about Mountain Jacks. Providentially, right across the street from that great restaurant is a greasy hamburger place. If the wind is blowing just right when you come out of Mountain Jacks, you can actually smell the aroma of that cheap fare. But you're never tempted to go across the street and eat there because you're so full of the good stuff.

Bitterness is like a cheap hamburger. It might do when you're starving, but why bother when there's such a superior alternative? Learn to handle bitter circumstances well. Root out sinful bitterness of heart and life. Enjoy the sweetness of God's presence and principles, and you'll never want to go back again.

» QUESTIONS FOR PERSONAL REFLECTION

1. What surprised you the most about the way the story of Ruth and Naomi ended? What are the lessons embedded in those surprises for you?

2. How do you see this story pointing to Jesus Christ? What are the similarities between Boaz and Jesus?

What does it mean to you that Jesus is your kinsman redeemer?

3. In your current situation, do you relate more closely to Ruth or Naomi? How do the principles in the book of Ruth help and direct you?

» QUESTIONS FOR GROUP DISCUSSION

1. What does the book of Ruth tell us about the character of God? Share with the group ways that God's goodness can impact your heart and life.

2. How have you seen God bless people who were seeking to faithfully follow him? What does that path look like? What should we do now if the blessings have not yet come?

3. Where does our view of eternity fit into this story? What if the bulk of our blessings occur in heaven? Is God's eternal goodness worth the wait?

Epilogue

Does Bitterness Have a Shelf Life?

As a thoughtful reader, you may have a nagging question about the Esau story. Without a doubt, at one time Esau's heart and life were consumed with bitterness toward his brother. Genesis 27:41 reports that "Esau bore a grudge against Jacob because of the blessing with which his father had blessed him; and Esau said to himself, 'The days of mourning for my father are near; then I will kill my brother Jacob.'" The New Testament commentary on his story says that he was an immoral and godless person who typified a root of bitterness that springs up, causes trouble, and defiles many (Heb. 12:15–17).

However, Esau's story doesn't end in Genesis 27. When he sees that his father instructs Jacob not to marry a Canaanite woman, Esau chooses to do that very thing (Gen. 28:8–9). In fulfillment of the Lord's prophecy to his mother, Rebekah (Gen. 25:23), Esau becomes a large nation that is a long-term enemy of God's covenant people.

The question revolves around Esau's behavior when Jacob returns after being away for twenty years serving his father-in-law, Laban. Jacob expected a fight with his bitter brother, but by all accounts Esau treated him well (Gen. 33).

So what happened to Esau's bitterness? The Bible is silent on that point, and therefore whatever we posit is speculation. One option is that Esau repented somewhere along the way. That explanation is unlikely, because the writer of Hebrews surely would have mentioned that detail when he used Esau as such a stark example of a root of bitter unbelief. Esau's marriage and the character of his descendants imply that he was always a profane, godless man.

Others might suggest that bitterness has a shelf life. The anger eventually subsides because "time heals all wounds," or so they say. There's nothing in the Word of God to justify that position. On the contrary, sin left unaddressed always comes back to the surface in ways that are more intense than before.

The more likely explanation is far more sinister. There's a twisted sense in which red-stuff living works, if by "works" we mean sin can be immediately, temporarily, and superficially gratifying. In Romans 1 parlance, God gives people up to their idolatrous desires. "He gave them up" is one of the most terrifying phrases in the Bible.

In Esau's case, his bitterness likely became his friend and closest companion. He found a way to make the root of unbelief work for him. He purposely married a Canaanite woman in direct disobedience to his parents' desires. He embraced red-stuff choices whenever and wherever he could. Ultimately his anger toward Jacob subsided because he did not care about the birthright. Seeking God's plan and God's covenant blessing mattered less to him with the passing of time. His bitterness became more comfortable and callous with each passing day.

If this understanding is correct, it heightens the urgency of the task. Finding a way to make your bitterness work is a recipe for disaster. Instead, seek to overcome sinful bitterness of heart and life before it becomes your new normal. Our sweet Savior stands ready to help you do just that.

Notes

Chapter 1 This Problem Is Bigger Than We Think

1. Lee Strobel, *God's Outrageous Claims*, 15.
2. Gary V. Smith, "*marah*," in *New International Dictionary of Old Testament Theology and Exegesis*, 2:1110.
3. Smith, "*marah*," 2:1111.
4. David McCullough, *The Pioneers*, 252.

Chapter 2 The Presence of Bitter Conditions

1. Smith, "*marah*," 2:1110–11.
2. Walter Kaiser, "Exodus," in the *Expositors Bible Commentary*, 2:373.
3. C. F. Keil and F. Delitzsch, "The Pentateuch," vol. 1 in *Commentary on the Old Testament*, 330.
4. McCullough, *The Pioneers*, 252.
5. C. H. Spurgeon, *Crossway Classic Commentaries, Psalms*, vol. 1, 159.
6. John MacArthur, *MacArthur Bible Commentary*, 622.
7. Referenced in Dave Furman, *Kiss the Wave*, 17. See also Furman, note 3, page 147 for historical background related to this reported quote.

Chapter 3 The Power of Bitter Lament

1. Mark Vroegop, *Dark Clouds, Deep Mercy*, 26.
2. J. Todd Billings, *Rejoicing in Lament*, 58–59.
3. Ken Barker and Waylon Bailey, *Micah, Nahum, Habakkuk, Zephaniah*, 277–78.
4. Vroegop, *Dark Clouds, Deep Mercy*, 31.
5. McCullough, *The Pioneers*, 252.
6. Vroegop, *Dark Clouds, Deep Mercy*, 44.

7. Vroegop, *Dark Clouds, Deep Mercy*, 48.
8. Vroegop, *Dark Clouds, Deep Mercy*, 48.
9. C. H. Spurgeon, quoted in J. I. Packer, *Knowing God*, 17–18.
10. Mark Vroegop, "Pastoral Lament for Tyler Trent," MarkVroegop.com, http://markvroegop.com/pastoral-lament-for-tyler-trent/.

Chapter 4 The Place of Bitter Tears

1. Bob Kellemen, *God's Healing for Life's Losses*, 24–25.
2. Craig Blomberg, "Matthew," *Commentary on the New Testament Use of the Old Testament*, 9.

Chapter 5 The Making of a Bitter Heart

1. John MacArthur, *Hebrews*, 408.

Chapter 6 Understanding and Embracing Fatherly Discipline

1. Stephen Ambrose, *Undaunted Courage*, 271.
2. Ambrose, *Undaunted Courage*, 300.
3. MacArthur, *Hebrews*, 385.
4. MacArthur, *Hebrews*, 385.
5. For more on this topic, see Steve Viars, *Loving Your Community*.

Chapter 8 Taming a Bitter Tongue

1. Melissa Denchak, "Flint Water Crisis: Everything You Need to Know," Natural Resources Defense Council, November 8, 2018, https://www.nrdc.org/stories/flint-water-crisis-everything-you-need-know.
2. Denchak, "Flint Water Crisis."
3. John MacArthur, *James*, 171.

Chapter 9 God Can Help You Overcome Bitterness

1. John Piper, *A Sweet and Bitter Providence*, 31.

Chapter 10 The Alternative of Sweet Faith

1. F. B. Huey Jr., "Ruth," *The Expositor's Bible Commentary*, 3:527.

Chapter 12 Embracing God's Sweetness

1. Brad Brandt and Eric Kress, *God in Everyday Life*, 125.
2. Brandt and Kress, *God in Everyday Life*, 125.

Bibliography

Adams, Jay. *What to Do When Anger Gets the Upper Hand*. Phillipsburg, NJ: P&R, 1992.

Ambrose, Stephen. *Undaunted Courage: Meriwether Lewis, Thomas Jefferson, and the Opening of the American West*. New York: Simon & Schuster, 1997.

Baker, Amy. *Getting to the Heart of Friendships*. Bemidji, MN: Focus, 2010.

Barker, Kenneth L., and Waylon Bailey. *Micah, Nahum, Habakkuk, Zephaniah*. Vol. 20 of *The New American Commentary*. Nashville: B&H, 1998.

Billings, J. Todd. *Rejoicing in Lament: Wrestling with Incurable Cancer and Life in Christ*. Grand Rapids: Brazos, 2015.

Blomberg, Craig. "Matthew" in *Commentary on the New Testament Use of the Old Testament*. Edited by D. A. Carson and G. K. Beale. Grand Rapids: Baker Academic, 2007.

Brandt, Brad, and Eric Kress. *God in Everyday Life: The Book of Ruth for Expositors and Biblical Counselors*. Woodlands, TX: Kress Christian Publications, 2007.

Brauns, Chris. *Unpacking Forgiveness: Biblical Answers for Complex Questions and Deep Wounds*. Wheaton: Crossway, 2008.

Furman, Dave. *Kiss the Wave: Embracing God in Your Trials*. Wheaton: Crossway, 2018.

Green, Rob. *Can We Talk? The Art of Relationship Building.* Greensboro, NC: New Growth, 2012.

———. *Forgiveness: Showing Grace When You Have Been Hurt.* Lafayette, IN: Faith Resources, n.d.

Hamilton, Victor. "*marah.*" Pages 528–29 in vol. 1 of *Theological Wordbook of the Old Testament.* Edited by R. Laird Harris, Gleason L. Archer Jr., and Bruce K. Waltke. 2 vols. Chicago: Moody, 1980.

Huey, F. B., Jr. "Ruth." In *The Expositor's Bible Commentary*, 509–49. Vol. 3. Grand Rapids: Zondervan, 1992.

Jones, Robert. *Anger: Calming Your Heart.* Phillipsburg, NJ: P&R, 2019.

———. *Freedom from Resentment: Stopping Hurts from Turning Bitter.* Greensboro, NC: New Growth, 2010.

———. *Pursuing Peace: A Christian Guide to Handling Our Conflict.* Wheaton: Crossway, 2012.

———. *Uprooting Anger: Biblical Help for a Common Problem.* Phillipsburg, NJ: P&R, 2005.

Kaiser, Walter. "Exodus." In *The Expositor's Bible Commentary*, 285–497. Vol. 2. Grand Rapids: Zondervan, 1990.

Keil, C. F., and F. Delitzsch. *The Pentateuch.* Vol. 1 of *Commentary on the Old Testament.* Repr. ed. Grand Rapids: Eerdmans, 1980.

Kellemen, Bob, and Kevin Carson, eds. *Biblical Counseling and the Church: God's Care through God's People.* Grand Rapids: Zondervan, 2015.

Kellemen, Bob, and Jeff Forrey, eds. *Scriptures and Counseling: God's Word for Life in a Broken World.* Grand Rapids: Zondervan, 2014.

Kellemen, Bob, and Steve Viars. *Christ-Centered Biblical Counseling: Changing Lives with God's Changeless Truth.* Rev. ed. Eugene, OR: Harvest House, 2020.

Kellemen, Robert. *God's Healing for Life's Losses: How to Find Hope When You're Hurting.* Winona Lake, IN: BMH, 2010.

MacArthur, John. *Hebrews.* The MacArthur New Testament Commentary Series. Chicago: Moody, 1983.

———. *James.* The MacArthur New Testament Commentary Series. Chicago: Moody, 1998.

————. *The MacArthur Bible Commentary*. Nashville: Thomas Nelson, 2005.

————. *The MacArthur Study Bible*. Nashville: Thomas Nelson, 2013.

Mack, Wayne. *Anger and Stress Management God's Way*. Phillipsburg, NJ: P&R, 2017.

McCullough, David. *The Pioneers: The Heroic Story of the Settlers Who Brought the American Ideal West*. New York: Simon & Schuster, 2019.

Newheiser, Jim. *Help! My Anger Is Out of Control*. Wapwallopen, PA: Shepherd Press, 2015.

Northrup, Solomon. *Twelve Years a Slave*. London: Hesperus Press, 2013.

Packer, J. I. *Knowing God*. Downers Grove, IL: InterVarsity, 1973.

Piper, John. *A Sweet and Bitter Providence: Sex, Race, and the Sovereignty of God*. Wheaton: Crossway, 2009.

Powlison, David. *Anger: Escaping the Maze*. Phillipsburg, NJ: P&R, 2000.

————. *Controlling Anger: Responding Constructively When Life Goes Wrong*. Greensboro, NC: New Growth, 2012.

————. *Good and Angry: Redeeming Anger, Irritation, Complaining, and Bitterness*. Greensboro, NC: New Growth, 2016.

Priolo, Lou. *Bitterness: The Root That Pollutes*. Phillipsburg, NJ: P&R, 2000.

————. *Resolving Conflict: How to Make, Disturb, and Keep Peace*. Phillipsburg, NJ: P&R, 2016.

Scott, Stuart, and Heath Lambert. *Counseling the Hard Cases: True Stories Illustrating the Sufficiency of God's Resources in Scripture*. Nashville: B&H Academic, 2012.

Smith, Gary V. *"marah"* in *New International Dictionary of Old Testament Theology and Exegesis*. 5 vols. Edited by Willem A. VanGemeren. Grand Rapids: Zondervan, 1997.

Spurgeon, Charles H. *Psalms, vol. 1*. Crossway Classic Commentaries. Wheaton: Crossway, 1993.

Strobel, Lee. *God's Outrageous Claims: Thirteen Discoveries That Can Transform Your Life*. Rev. ed. Grand Rapids: Zondervan, 2016.

Tripp, Paul. *War of Words: Getting to the Heart of Your Communication Struggles*. Phillipsburg, NJ: P&R, 2001.

Viars, Steve. *Loving Your Community: A Handbook for Community-Based Ministry*. Grand Rapids: Baker Books, 2020.

———. *Putting Your Past in Its Place: Moving Forward in Freedom and Forgiveness*. Eugene, OR: Harvest House, 2011.

———. *Redeeming Your Painful Past: Present Grace, Future Hope*. Greensboro, NC: New Growth, 2012.

Vroegop, Mark. *Dark Clouds, Deep Mercy: Discovering the Grace of Lament*. Wheaton: Crossway, 2019.

Welch, Ed. *A Small Book about a Big Problem: Meditations on Anger, Patience, and Peace*. Greensboro, NC: New Growth, 2017.

Stephen Viars (MDiv, Grace Theological Seminary; DMin, Westminster Theological Seminary) has served as a pastor and biblical counselor at Faith Church and Faith Biblical Counseling Ministries in Lafayette, Indiana, since 1987. He is a frequent speaker at conferences, colleges, and seminaries in the United States and abroad. In addition to overseeing the staff and ministries at Faith, he also serves on the boards of the Association of Certified Biblical Counselors, the Biblical Counseling Coalition, Vision of Hope, and the Faith Community Development Corporation. The author of *Loving Your Community* and *Putting Your Past in Its Place*, he and his wife, Kris, have been married since 1982 and have three children and three grandchildren.

ARE YOU AND YOUR CHURCH MAKING A DIFFERENCE IN YOUR COMMUNITY?

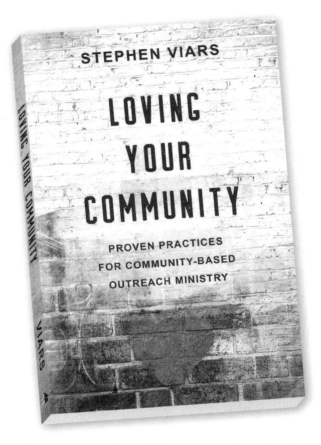

Drawing on more than thirty years of service to the community surrounding Faith Church in Indiana, pastor Stephen Viars shows you how to develop a dynamic, giving relationship with your community, one in which your natural response to needs is "Yes! How can we help?"

For More on
Faith Ministries

At **FAITHLAFAYETTE.ORG** visitors can learn more about our diverse programs and outreach options.

Visit **FAITHLAFAYETTE.ORG/COMMUNITY** to learn more about our three community centers and the Hartford Hub.

Within our community ministry pages, you can also learn more about our Community Development Corporation, Car Works program, Strategic Ministry Plan, collaborative partnerships, and **MUCH MORE!**

Visit us on Facebook:

@FaithEastCommunityCenter
@FaithWestCommunityCenter
@NorthEndCommunityCenter
@HartfordHubLafayette